An Andrew Crozi

ANDREW CROZIER was born in 1943 and was educa... College and Christ's College, Cambridge. In 1964, the same year in which he founded the Ferry Press, he was awarded a Fulbright Scholarship to study at the State University of New York, Buffalo, where he was taught by Charles Olson and made contact with the almost-forgotten poet Carl Rakosi, prompting Rakosi's return to writing. In 1998, Crozier published an edition of Rakosi's early poems. Crozier's first collection, *Loved Litter of Time Spent* (1967), was published while he was in the United States. On his return to England, he studied for a PhD at the University of Essex under Donald Davie, before taking up a post at the University of Sussex in 1973, where he remained until his retirement as Professor of English in 2005. He founded two journals, *The English Intelligencer* and the *Wivenhoe Park Review*, later the *Park Review*, while continuing to publish his own and others' poetry in Ferry Press editions. He wrote extensive literary criticism and in 1983 co-edited the influential anthology *A Various Art*, published by Carcanet Press. His collected poems were published in 1985 with the title *All Where Each Is* (Allardyce, Barnett). Andrew Crozier died in 2008.

IAN BRINTON studied at Gonville and Caius College, Cambridge, before going on to a career in English teaching. He was Head of English at Leeds Grammar School, Sevenoaks School and Dulwich College before retiring in 2009. He was an editor of *The Use of English* from 2003 to 2011. Ian Brinton has written books on Dickens and Emily Bronte, and is the author of *Contemporary Poetry since 1990* (Cambridge University Press, 2009) and the editor of *A Manner of Utterance: The Poetry of J.H. Prynne* (Shearsman, 2009).

Drawing of Andrew Crozier by Fielding Dawson, New York 1965
Reproduced by permission

An Andrew Crozier Reader

edited with an introduction by
Ian Brinton

CARCANET

First published in Great Britain in 2012 by
Carcanet Press Limited
Alliance House
Cross Street
Manchester M2 7AQ

www.carcanet.co.uk

A CIP catalogue record for this book is available from the British Library
ISBN 978 1 84777 100 1

The publisher acknowledges financial assistance from Arts Council England

Typeset by XL Publishing Services, Tiverton
Printed and bound in England by SRP Ltd, Exeter

CONTENTS

II Essex and Keele

Walking on Grass

FROM THE ROOT

WALKING ON GRASS

III *Printed Circuit* to *The Veil Poem*

Printed Circuit

Neglected Information

VIII 'Free Running Bitch'

IX Resting on Laurels

ILLUSTRATIONS

ACKNOWLEDGEMENTS

I wish to acknowledge the untiring assistance offered to me by Andrew Crozier's wife Jean, and by his brother, Philip; without their generous cooperation it would have been impossible to put this volume together. In addition, the assistance given by Derek Slade in putting together the bibliography has been invaluable. I also wish to dedicate this book to my wife, Kay, whose patience while I have been closeted in my study has been a hallmark of her support for the whole venture.

Ian Brinton

INTRODUCTION

Soon after Andrew Crozier's death in April 2008 the *Independent* published an obituary by Nicholas Johnson, himself a prominent poet and founder of Etruscan Books. Subtitled 'Poet and poet's champion', Johnson's piece pointed to the extraordinary way in which Crozier had fostered the world of poetry in England from the mid-1960s to his premature death soon after his retirement from the University of Sussex:

> At just 20 years old, the poet Andrew Crozier began to nurture and revitalise – through his small-press publishing – a rich terrain of first American, then British, modernist poetry. This had a rapid effect for his peers, principally those associated with the Cambridge School. Crozier disseminated, circulated and, with what became an increasingly anonymous generosity, encouraged and stimulated countless writers and visual artists. If he partly achieved this as an editor, archivist, publisher and teacher, it was quietly reflective of his precise gift as a poet.
>
> Now his poetry is out of print.

In the two years before his death this last point was a matter of some serious debate, and there was some important correspondence between Andrew Crozier and Michael Schmidt about the possibility of producing a 'Selected Writings' which might include both poetry and some prose. In his response to one of Schmidt's letters, Crozier, who had only recently retired from academic life, provides some interesting insights into what he was working on right up until the end:

> 2nd May 2006
>
> Retirement itself will, surely, have consequences for writing of any sort, although I have no strong sense of what is likely. This is relevant to my perplexity about how to respond to your invitation. Hitherto I have responded to expressions of interest in publishing a new collected edition of my poems by saying that to do so seemed premature while I had rather little to add to *All Where Each Is*, and difficult to justify. (Indeed, difficult to justify to myself although that book has been out of print for some

while.) What I've separately thought is that the situation requires the publication of a further separate collection, including 'Free Running Bitch' (previously published in *Conductors of Chaos*), before anything else.

I've made these points to other publishers more tersely than I do here, hence my responses have, reasonably enough, as well as correctly, been taken as refusals. I don't think, however, that this response is either appropriate or sufficient when the expression of interest comes from you and Carcanet. Hence my perplexity about how to respond; you will appreciate, I do hope, that the perplexity is with reference to my situation.

Since your invitation is couched in terms of 'writings' perhaps I should say something about critical writings, not the least because some pieces of critical writing are foremost in my mind at present. I have in hand essays on John James (for a collection on him) and on Basil King's *Mirage*. Looming over both these, and most of all else, is a long essay on Harry Roskolenko, a minor but symptomatic poet of the 1930s and 1940s. (He began as one of Zukofsky's 'Objectivists', and by the end of the 1930s was the American arm of the New Apocalypse. Add to this that he was part of the Left Opposition – i.e. Trotskyish – working undercover in the CPUSA and, from my point of view, he has everything going for him.) I give this detail in order to point out that my critical writing is miscellaneous, as it stands, but also, notionally at least, some of it preliminary to separately developed monographs on the 'Objectivists' and the New Apocalypse.

A few days later I received a letter from Andrew which again discussed the possibility of his work being put back into the public eye:

11th May

Your point that my work is unobtainable is not lost on me, indeed it is one I can't avoid as an emphatic consideration whenever (unfrequently) I contemplate my position qua poet. It doesn't outweigh, in the balance of wishes and intentions, my hesitancies about republication tout court. I don't want to appear, not the least to myself, as resting on my laurels. Were I to abjure poetry, or were I dead, the work could be left to make its own way as helped by others. The second of these circumstances is not an otiose form of words: publication can seem like a symbolic death, a book like a monument, with damaging as well as painful effects.

> There is another side to this, of course, connected with the vanity of not wishing to appear an historical figure. Enough said the better!

In an article for the *London Review of Books* in July 1997, Jeremy Harding highlighted some of the essential ingredients of a Crozier poem and made it abundantly clear why this poetry most certainly should be back in print:

> In his easy vernacular, Crozier tamps down language with the skill of a painter achieving a rare equivalence of terms on the canvas. Often, too, we find an observed action or a local detail quickly entailed to something larger and simpler: the pattern of day and night, seasonal change, or the slippage of light and shadow. This has the effect of ascribing thought and emotion not to the speaking subject (the poet) but to the processes of the poem. A deceptively shambling manner, with its cat's cradles of clauses, promiscuous participles and other equivocations of grammar spreads the load of the bigger themes and adds to a sense of forms thinking aloud, in a number of voices. Once again, the approach is painterly: the figurative elements of a typical Crozier poem are briefly acknowledged and then abstracted by the momentum of its composition into the broadest space it can construe. The result is extraordinary.

This collage-like inventiveness was noted in Peter Riley's *Guardian* obituary from July 2008, as was Crozier's proposition that 'a poem should be constantly and freshly conceived as a construct of language which achieves beauty through a fidelity to the actual'. His meditations on landscape and on the intimacy of the domestic world are 'expressed in a bared honesty which is the result of considerable discipline'. Riley went on to present a vivid picture of that 'historical figure' Andrew Crozier had wryly abjured:

> From the outset, Crozier worked to bring practitioners together. In 1966 he founded *The English Intelligencer*, a 'worksheet' circulated among some 30 poets to exchange knowledge of their current activities without worrying too much about finished poems, and from 1964 onwards ran The Ferry Press, which published first or early books of many important British poets in carefully designed editions, frequently with covers designed by then little-known artists, including Patrick Caulfield and Michael

Craig-Martin. He collaborated further, in special illustrated editions of his own poetry, with artists such as Ian Tyson, Tom Phillips, and his own brother, Philip Crozier.

His criticism was important, but remains as yet scattered in periodicals and anthologies, and some of his projects were never completed. The stress was again on sweeping the board clean and examining the history afresh: what took place, what was produced and what its value might be, and this naturally resulted in reversals of received positions, and the rescuing of forgotten poets, which became almost a speciality of his.

In a letter Michael Schmidt wrote to Crozier in July 2006 he emphasised the importance of this critical work:

> I have the highest regard possible for your critical essays. They dig far deeper and uncover far more than most of the critical writings of writers I admire in our generation. It is the carefulness with which the argument proceeds, the almost Ridingesque insistence on precision, that makes your work such a tonic (fortunately the style is much more readable than hers!).

The evidence of Andrew Crozier's commitment to the setting straight of records is to be found in the immense amount of work he left unfinished, the pulling together of which will become an interesting and important task for future scholars. A brief outline of the sort of material he was involved with was presented in the May 2006 letter to Schmidt quoted above, and some further details were given in the letter to me, in which he talks of his commitment to finishing three pieces of work:

> Two of these are no more than occasionalistic, but the other one, on Harry Roskolenko, raises the possibility of a unified treatment of the Objectivists and the New Apocalypse. Roskolenko isn't an important poet, but he opens a number of issues that might otherwise seem irrelevant, in particular the connections between Objectivism and Proletarian writing, and the implications of Zukofsky's negative, but very carefully weighed verdict on Hart Crane. Crane's influence elsewhere, specifically on Dylan Thomas and his imitators, then becomes the antithesis of Objectivism's occlusion/collapse during the 1930s.
>
> This is time-consuming stuff, partly because it means pecking away at the contemporary significances of such events as the

> Reichstag fire trial, partly because Roskolenko left a massive, but dispersed archive. There are a few paragraphs to add to what I've already written, but my presentation of him so far is as someone who passed through different sets of circumstances, and doesn't address the possibility of drawing them together.

The purpose of this *Andrew Crozier Reader* is to bring back into the public eye the gifted poet and the untiring promoter of poetry's importance, to allow readers to judge for themselves the extraordinary range of work spanning forty years. Nicholas Johnson's term, 'poet's champion', refers not only to the central importance of the anthology, *A Various Art*, edited by Crozier and Tim Longville in 1987, in which the exciting new world of what was happening in poetry found a decisive and attractive presentation, but also to the fact that Crozier contributed an anthology of 'Ten English Poets' to *New Directions 32*, 'An International Anthology of Prose & Poetry'.

When Andrew Crozier retired after some thirty years at Sussex he made it abundantly clear that it was in order to start new ventures:

> Have I mentioned that I took early retirement at the start of the academic year? The effect is of a protracted intellectual spring clean, a mixture of exhilaration and remorse.

Two months later he referred to 'the abundant reading time' afforded to him by retirement:

> I am under the necessity of disposing of a lot of books, and there are cases where it becomes necessary to reread (even to read) before reaching the fateful decision. In many more cases, of course, the decisions are easy and with a sort of jubilation at no more of authors x, y, and z.

What is undoubted here is the continuation of his work of discrimination and judgement, a refusal to slide along with the readily accepted, an angularity of quiet determination which is a reflection upon a lifetime's achievement.

A NOTE ON THE TEXT

The texts of most of the poems reproduced here are taken from the first published collected edition, *All Where Each Is* (Allardyce, Barnett, 1985) unless otherwise stated. The text of 'Free Running Bitch' is as it appears in *Conductors of Chaos* (edited by Iain Sinclair; Picador, 1996). Crozier's reviews and prose writing are reproduced here as they appeared on first publication, with only minor modifications to ensure consistency of style. An archive of the papers and letters of Andrew Crozier is held at the Cambridge University Library. Private letters from Crozier to the editor remain with him.

I
CAMBRIDGE AND NEW YORK

In an interview with Peter Ryan titled 'From Missile Crisis to English Intelligencer'*, published in* Don't Start Me Talking *(2006), Andrew Crozier talked about his early reading of modern poetry in his last two years at Dulwich College, before he left in July 1961 to read English at Christ's College, Cambridge. He referred to work by Norman MacCaig and Christopher Logue, as well as the American John Crowe Ransom, but it was not until his final year at Cambridge that he became deeply involved with the world of American modernism that was to influence his own work extensively over the following years.*

During my last two or three years at school [1958–61] I began reading modern poetry; the first modern British poet I read seriously, borrowing the books from the public library, was Norman MacCaig. (The other one I remember reading in the same way was Christopher Logue.) So I can remember reading *A Common Grace* by Norman MacCaig when it was published and also Christopher Logue's translations of Pablo Neruda, and a volume of Logue's own poems published by Villiers Press. My reason for writing poems I think had to do with, perhaps I read a lot of poetry at the time, but up till the summer of 1963 I did not consider that writing poems might be a serious business, in other words it was a talent or a competence that people possessed at which I essayed my own abilities. I think that when I first tried to write poems I was interested first of all in what my contemporaries did, which impressed me considerably by its competence because they actually produced a finished text. I refer to undergraduate poets in my own years at Cambridge, people who were writing poems then and publishing them in university magazines, who no longer write poems and whose names need no longer be remembered. The second influence had to do with poems I was then reading, and my understanding of poetry as it was undertaken in England at that time was partial. I might be aware of Christopher Logue and Norman MacCaig, for example, but I couldn't put them onto any kind of map together. I also read American poets and I can remember being interested while I was still at school by John Crowe Ransom. That should be seen in the context in which I read, say, Yeats and also Hopkins as modern poets, but there were no co-ordinates by which to relate Ransom or MacCaig, or for that matter Logue, to those other poets I was led to read by teachers at school. At the same time, in my first two years at university I was more directly involved in activities not concerned with poetry. I was concerned with film societies and I considered the possibility of making films after I left Cambridge. I was fairly closely involved in the anti-nuclear protest movement at the time. I certainly felt that the envisageable future in 1961–62 was not a very distant place: I had a very short-term view of the future because I think that I imagined that there would be destruction of the world in which I lived by nuclear war. What brought that frame of mind to an end was the Cuban crisis in 1962. There was no Armageddon and things resolved themselves in terms of power politics, which was an explanation of the world which up till then my politics had not led me to expect. And so I withdrew fairly consciously from political activity, from serious involvement in looking at and writing about films, and in a certain kind of hiatus in my life at that point, associated with an illness during which I read Charles Olson and Robert Duncan and William Carlos Williams, I brought myself to the point at which, by the end of my second year at university, I was interested in nothing other than poetry, and so I would date my intentional involvement with poetry from the summer of 1963 and my earliest retained, published poems from that summer.

Later in the same interview Crozier referred to being aware of:

an antagonism in the poetic world, in England especially, between the advocates of a formal prosody and their adversaries, less clearly defined, who would be the then contemporary inheritors of the technical aspects of early 20th century modernism. So that, to pin this down more precisely, I read very carefully the second *New Lines* anthology edited by Robert Conquest, which had a long introductory essay by Conquest which made a number of quite prescriptive comments about the formal organisation of poems, including an argument that there was no reason not to write in metrical forms because any restricted prosodic form nevertheless offered if not an infinite variety, certainly a very high order of variety because of the possibility of variation within a set form. My recollection is that I was not particularly convinced by his arguments, although I did not altogether understand why they did not convince me. As against the *New Lines* mode I was looking more to the example of American writers whom I had been reading since my first term at Cambridge, and the Donald Allen anthology, *The New American Poetry, 1945–60*, gave access to more recent American poets, principally Charles Olson, although I was also very much impressed by John Wieners and Edward Dorn who also published in that anthology.

These ideas were more formally laid out in a review Crozier published in the October 1963 issue of Granta, *in which he looked closely at both Robert Conquest's* New Lines 2 *and the Faber edition of* Five American Poets *which had been compiled by Ted Hughes and Thom Gunn. In the review he suggested that the poets included in Conquest's anthology 'are our orthodoxy, not our rebels' and noted that the work of most of Conquest's poets showed a total separation of form and content: 'Maybe by ignoring form (in fact just accepting iambics, rhyme and periodic stanza patterns) they think they can pay attention to their content; but, their content is trivial.' Crozier went on to quote from section two of Charles Olson's 'Projective Verse', the whole of which had appeared in the sixth section of Donald Allen's anthology:*

> It comes to this: the use of a man, by himself and thus by others, lies in how he convinces his relation to nature, that force to which he owes his somewhat small existence. If he sprawl, he shall find little to sing but himself, and shall sing, nature has such paradoxical ways, by way of artificial forms outside himself. But if he stays inside himself, if he is contained within his nature as he is participant in the larger force, he will be able to listen, and his hearing through himself will give him secrets objects share. And by an inverse law his shapes will make their own way... For a man's problem, the moment he takes speech up in all its seriousness, is to give his work his seriousness, a seriousness sufficient to cause the thing he makes to try to take its place alongside the things of nature.

Crozier added:

> The point is this: by the adherence to an iambic line, their use of rhyme, and their use of stanzaic patterns that impose an arbitrary pattern on the poem once the first stanza has been composed (even supposing that it has not been taken ready made from a

> source other than what the poet might have to say) the 'New Lines' poets have closed their poetry to most experience; they have little to say to us. What they give us in place of their experience is a dilute poeticism, so many words slotted into a pattern, a pursuit of metaphor and simile as interesting in themselves.

In these poems from New Lines 2, *in which objects were always defining something or other rather than being allowed to exist in their own right, Crozier saw 'a disabling force which predisposes the poet to a thinness of presented experience, and a lack of humility in his approach (as poet) to the external world'. In contrast to this 'disabling force' Crozier's review directed the reader to some of William Stafford's work from the Faber selection of American poets:*

> William Stafford exists within that community of American poetry from William Carlos Williams on; he makes use of the ends of his lines. His poems have all a sense of place, a sense of specific activity, in time... details exist as colouring, admittedly; but it is the quality of William Stafford's colour that is important, the little quotidian things he uses, and with respect.

In a letter to me dated 18 February 2006 Crozier noted, 'It sometimes seems to me that my ideas have hardly moved on from the review...'.The pursuit of his interest in Donald Allen's anthology was prompted by his meeting with J.H. Prynne in the Lent Term of 1963, when Crozier was studying at Christ's College and his Director of Studies, John Rathmell, sent him to see Prynne 'as to an oracle on such matters' (letter to the present editor, 12 September 2006). In either late 1963 or early 1964 Crozier showed some of his early poems to Prynne, including 'Drill Poem' and 'Getting ready to come back here', both of which were later to be published in Prospect 6, *a Cambridge magazine of which Prynne was editor at the time. Prynne's response to 'Drill Poem', in a letter from January 1964, had been encouraging:*

> My feeling is that there is an accuracy of placement to be found, that the smallest shifts of metric are crucial to it, that these 'random' fragments are a clandestine beginning. 'Drill Poem' is a success with the possible exception of 'wavers' which I think is the wrong word. Wrong shape and the sound against the working grain.

This 'clandestine beginning' soon became a part of Crozier's first volume of poems, Train Rides, Poems from '63 & '64. *Published in 1968, it contained an afterword of explanation:*

> I have called these poems *Train Rides* which come from a period of my life when whatever I was feeling could not be attached to a particular place. This may be a belated recognition, but it was no coincidence that most of these poems were written on the train when I, eluding the uncertainty of location in any one place, could recognise where I had come from in the prospect of somewhere to go to. Which implied other people and selves also. It is equally no coincidence that they were the same two poems which, in each instance, avoided these conditions.
>
> These are the poems that remain from 1963 and the early months of 1964 when I first wrote with any measure of intention. Some of them have been published in the *Evergreen Review, Granta, Prospect, Snow,* and *Tlaloc.* I wish to dedicate them all to my brother Philip.

-o0o-

Train Rides

1 *Name & Nature*

Man's energies have such bounds
he turns in
                    shores up his force
looking out   must see return
before he venture
          the receptivity and going out
          of itself of one
          and the embrace and possession by the other
          the mingling of these two together
          has its analogies
the cost is reckoned and restrains
though unaccustom breeds its own limits,
and the gift conditional, part of
himself.
The world is outside
actions
          cannot be recovered
and though strength might lie in confidence

to think of resources discourages
            gesturing outwards to
            -wards another, to embrace
                encircling receive and
            take into possession
has its analogies with
            breeding in nature and
            marriage among human kind.

2 *Drill Poem*

Nearly my arm's length
its grey mass heavy in my hand
feels good   working on the ceiling
held vertical the bit spins
level with my eyes and
head jammed against concrete
for balance

pull the trigger, press the catch, ram
the bit against the mark wavers
then a fine spray of dust falls
in my face, sweat
runs through my brow
my arms shake
            my ears
    sing

3 *Getting Ready To Come Back Here*

More to be learnt
looking from the window of the train
    riding through north London into the fields
than from prolonged scrutiny of the
            others in the buffet car
It is
            the traverse
    its instant glimpse of man
suspended in his action
  :the fat railwayman creased over his uniform

  :the linesman blowing on his horn
or the Gérard Philippe character? smiles
extended index touch-
        touching eyebrow lip and cheek

4

                    Your smell
(I said)
lingers on
after you, and I
take it to bed with me
it permeates
the sheets
        you cling
to me across this
distance
              the separation
is as nothing.

5

You turn
        from me
toward the window
head bent & cupped in your palm
you hide behind
              your hair
or are hidden

It's dark outside, the train
moves through the rain

two splashes darken
your green sleeve
            you hide
your tears

6 *Early Morning, Night Sorting Shift*

How we left
the tea break
not returning to work but to go

walking across Parker's Piece
and through town, down
to the Mill

comes back
crossing the Piece again
how the water sounded
in the dark
It gets louder
I said
as you get nearer the mill race
and subsides
when you cross
to the other parapet
the water churning beneath the bridge
beneath you   to see

white foam
eddying
across the pond

7

Young men from old poets should learn
honour, love
their craft
comes not of itself
but of love and
honour paid

the songs
the old men sing

•

how softly
the song
carries
across the Atlantic

8 *The Lunatic*

I used to look at the moon, sweetheart, when you
were difficult
to see if she were full

but tonight, 12.30
   I walk home lit   .   the sky is bright

my hand on your breast
was dark as
you looked up, saying
You look
etc.

looking at dark on light

how the moon is in
the sky behind
the clouds

9

All across this country standing
water in the fields
after the sudden snow
this March has brought inland these
birds – peewits and gulls
and a floppy, large
brown bird I don't know
                    all standing
in the water wading
the fields

10

Daily, and
it gets worse
every day   something more
to speak of

to whom
though does one speak
and of what, or where
to pinpoint discourse
what are we to do   what
can we

A note on the train, January 1966

A ploughed field, on a slope; I would only write what feelings they arouse into a notebook. The revealed formation, a rich brown Hertfordshire dirt is the enduring feature of the landscape. Otherwise there are scrubby fields, golf links; towns like Stevenage and Welwyn; Elm trees, cabbages.

Winter discloses the surface articulation of the Earth. There are dashes of chalk across the dark ploughland, and the trees, with branches that attenuate to a careful twigginess, occur in groups in random-looking dispersion.

The slopes become predominantly chalky, and among the bare fields are strips of woodland in which the Beech and the Birch mix with the Elm. The landscape opens and the fields are larger with hedges inbetween, as the train gathers speed.

-oOo-

In March 1964 Crozier went on to edit an American Supplement to Granta. *Unlike Charles Tomlinson's anthology which had appeared in* the Review *that January, this short collection of work by Denise Levertov, Robert Duncan, Ed Dorn, Fielding Dawson, Larry Eigner, Douglas Woolf, Robert Kelly, John Wieners, Robert Creeley and Ron Loewinsohn was not intended as a Black Mountain feature as such and was largely based on the Donald Allen anthology. The supplement opens with a letter from Charles Olson to George Butterick in which he uses the phrase 'to freshen our sense of the language we do have'. Crozier's own introductory note reiterates the importance of this:*

I don't see any point in writing a formal intro. to this collection. The cohesion is there, and if you don't see it, go back to Olson's letter: 'freshen our sense of the language we do have', he says. And read again. Then let these notes help you read more.

The importance of Charles Olson for Crozier was to do with conviction, a belief in the central importance of being a poet. He expanded on this in the interview with Peter Ryan, 'From Missile Crisis to English Intelligencer*':*

I think that my interest in becoming a poet had to do with finding a mode for making sense of and placing together a complete or a self-completing scheme of being alive. In other words...it became an appropriate project to be a poet at the time when my knowledge of poetry began to seem to hold out some fairly complete image in world experience. In my case that had to do particularly with reading Charles Olson. I read the essay 'Human Universe' probably a month or so after my turnaround following the Cuban crisis, and it made a very immediate kind of sense to my rather political mental set, which at the same time was depoliticised because it was not preoccupied with action or political involvement in any way. I'm not attempting to say why I might now suggest that Olson is important if I were talking about him to one of my students. I'm talking about the rather occluded sense of myself in the world that I feel I was equipped with in the early Sixties, within which reading Olson occurred as some kind of light, because it was associated both with the failure or the cessation of one series of life interests, life experiences, and the possible burgeoning of another... It's not the case that I read the Americans and felt that here was an example to be imitated... They were examples of the poetic existence... I don't think that I would have thought about being a poet as opposed to occasionally writing pieces of verse had I not thought about the possibility of being a poet as all-consuming preoccupation, and the Americans suggested, through the very narrow representation of their work that was afforded to me in London and Cambridge at that time, that being a poet was in some way a full-time serious activity.

Crozier also referred in that interview to the complete seriousness of being a poet: 'Olson, and the other poets whom I saw as ancillaries of Olson's, provided examples not of things which could be imitated but of a disposition towards writing which filled the business of writing with human seriousness, something like that.'

While at Cambridge Crozier met Donald Davie and was invited to work on his interests with a team of American and English graduates in the Department of Comparative Literature in the new University of Essex at Wivenhoe Park, which was due to open in October 1965. With this prospect ahead of him he spent the time between graduating from Cambridge in 1964 and June 1965 at State University New York (SUNY), Buffalo, studying under Olson and financing himself there with a teaching fellowship. Although that fellowship was tenable for three years and he could have obtained an American PhD, he had agreed to bring home the fruit of his researches to continue at Essex. Davie's comments in support of his application for a grant for his studies at Essex stress the measure of regard he had for this young man: 'it is as important to us to have him around next year as it is important to him' (letter to the poet's mother, Kathleen Crozier).

In April 1965 at SUNY Crozier produced a foolscap anthology of Thirteen English Poets, *titled* SUM, *which reflected his clear sense of a dialogue taking place between poets of the two countries. If Donald Allen's Grove Press anthology of* New American Poetry *was intended to make the little islanders aware of what was taking place in the US, Crozier was equally determined that the innovative poetry, far distant from the world of* New Lines 2, *that was being written in England should be presented to his American hosts. The selection included Charles Tomlinson, John James, Gael Turnbull, Michael Shayer, Michael Mead, Roy Fisher, Anselm Hollo, Tom Raworth, Jim Burns, John Temple, Basil Bunting, Tom Pickard and Crozier himself. Prynne was clearly intending to offer something for the publication, but the pressure of work prevented him; on 17 April 1965 he wrote to Crozier: 'So, I wasn't able to send something (as I wished & would have liked) for SUM'. One of Crozier's own inclusions was 'What Spokes and to What Hub?', which was later to be published in the substantial volume* Loved Litter of Time Spent, *with a cover designed by Fielding Dawson and an introduction by Prynne. These Buffalo poems were privately printed in May 1967 in an edition of 100 copies, 'not for sale with appreciation to English Department, State University of New York at Buffalo SUMBOOKS', prefaced by Prynne's introduction. The title of the book was a phrase taken from the novel* The River Slea *by Anthony Ward, a Research Fellow at St John's in 1961 and the editor of* Prospect 5. Prospect 6, *which had included Crozier's 'Drill Poem', had also contained an extract from Ward's work in progress, which clearly struck a chord with the young Crozier.*

With the exception of 'How Does It Go', the selection here from this volume is the one made by Crozier himself for All Where Each Is.

-o0o-

Loved Litter of Time Spent

There are certain movements in time which are unimportant, except that they do this one thing, setting a period and point of return almost like an oscillic reflex. Tuned to this is the space one has, the possible as it really comes over, day by day. It is quite plausible to take this as a condition for accuracy: which is what Andrew has done here. Each piece has a simple lunar equinox, if you shake water in a cup the seam will hold itself, and only your hand will feel the outward sway. Just where these poems were written is anyone's guess, but the arbitrary limits of title are for this purpose the condition of Buffalo during this time, syntax commensurate with the ethnic and other slight facts of the case. Not where you get to but what it's possible to include, absolute limit of presence is the line set down. I happen to find the sequence here offset to something like weather, or sentiment, all bound to a distraction of feeling; I trust that, as it seems just apt to infer the changed cruelties of the new world. As most things are mostly new, and as the words go out into the air, taking a new life with them, to frost or vapour on the cheek we almost touch. Summer 1965 was really too hot, nobody goes there anymore.

J.H. Prynne

The Americans

The Americans go by in their cars
I am standing at the bus stop

I go by in Fred's van
Three Negroes are standing at the bus stop

(At the Salvation Army
Three floors of junk)

In their insulated houses
In their insulating cars

The Americans stand too far apart
As their houses are far apart

No one stands in the street

Numbers Are Adjectives: Counting Cats

One Two Three
my natural numbers
(Campion's song –
'the proper ordering')
is syntax, the ordinals
Four Five Six
(ordained?) follow so
perception : proportion
two cats or three?
Seven Eight and Nine
increase of one half
but eight cats or nine?
four twos or three threes or
wait till I've counted.

A Judy

She comes to me
now, she walks into the bar
placing her
feet, almost
a nautical roll
a slow way of walking / a tight step
from the hips, not the shoulders
she hunches, yes? in the cold
to raise her collar so
it warms her chin

this is Steve's wife, she is tall and
slender   Penny, Hello   she said
she was slim too, I laughed

The Elders

– know each other yet
do not touch, making
gentle inquiries, each the other
seeing, so separate

an old man disappointed
(did he ever have hopes?) accepting
that disappointment becomes him almost
a decadence he articulates so clearly
the Academy its viciousness

the other's Politics
(do you hear him?) he speaks
it, the placeman, it is
intelligence discriminates
the sole locus of struggle we
have
        – to be followed

What Spokes, and to What Hub?

There are many parts I have not been to, but start
from Gloucester, coming from Fishguard that morning, and
                                                                                    eventually
from Courtmacsherry, leaving in a rainstorm on the afternoon bus
thirty miles north to Cork to take the night ferry
                                                                        walked that
morning into Milfordhaven, only Council lorries on the road
carrying earth to some site off the main route
              a manifest regret
                                        a short way
out of the town with a travelling grocer, a fine thing to be
a poet, his son at Cardiff training to be an engineer
                                                                        fast to Carmarthen
I could only buy ice creams and walk out of the town
a deep valley where the road branches east and
north to Lampeter, rain and more Council works
I rode a lorry from there a week before
coming south from the Williams's at Llandecwyn nr. Talsarnau
                    I follow east
towards London, my home
with a traveller making for Devon
the next night, so far around the Bristol Channel
we swung south towards Cardiff on a call, his day's
work, then I brought him back north
across the Carmarthenshire mountains, the Brecon Beacons

high grasslands where no one lives, no sheep are grazed even
a quern the size of a mill wheel
is lost there
Yvor Pritchard my father's friend
came back and could not find it
a proximate horizon the hills arch
a narrow sky you climb steadily towards
back to the main route, turning east to
run through the little marcher towns, Brecon, Monmouth
past a signpost: To Usk
ten miles away
I could ask to stop and turn down there, easily
find her family in a town of 2000, find at least
where she went
but that was sixteen months ago, and I did not stop, it is
even further away as I remember her
in Brighton, spending Easter at Kimbo's place
and it snowed as I went through Redhill
Was it she came to these States this summer? to ride to Los Angeles
her name, her gesture, her age
I know one her like now –
is there attraction in resemblance?
I rode on to Gloucester.

A Spring Song

The little lambs
the bloody cauls

the ewes drop
both, as they crop

the new green
grass the Spring

brings mushrooms
too, and the dykes

rush full in
the sluice

a lamb floats
on its back

its belly
bloated its

wool still has
the tight coil of

the new born

-o0o-

In a letter which Peter Riley sent to Crozier in January 1967 he referred to a folder of poems which contained one about Romney Marsh, and suggested that 'if you put it in the Intelligencer *I'll write a reply to it, or rather a work on the same subject following from yours. I didn't take a copy of it, but remember something of it, and I'd like to see it again'. 'On Romney Marsh' and Riley's sequel 'From Romney Marsh' consequently appeared on pp. 217–19 of the magazine's First Series, with the opening word of Riley's*

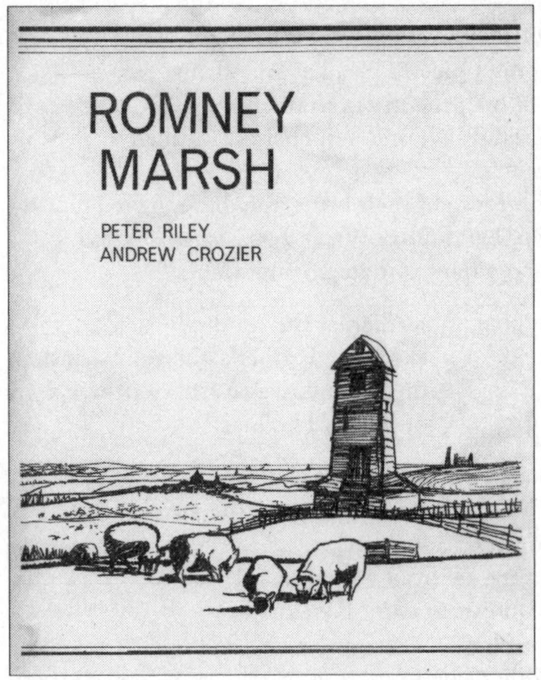

title suggesting how one poem had arisen 'from' the other. A measure of Crozier's valuation of the two linking poems, the second acting as a response to the first, was evidenced soon after by the separate publication of the two poems by Ferry Press in May 1967 in an edition of 100 copies with a cover design drawn by Crozier's mother, Kathleen.

-o0o-

On Romney Marsh [written December 1964, revised January 1967]

The sheep on Romney Marsh
have probably been there since the sea withdrew
or at least since the salt was drained and the land
become pasturage
                    cut through with dykes
to hold the land high, and so low, to walk across
in series of right angles
seeking the plank bridges, you might go
a long way from your way

          the sheep at least have been there
          long enough to be a known breed, remain
          the use of their wool

or just mutton grazing the fields below
the rise of the Queen's Head at Icklesham
as you look over the marsh to the humps
on which stand Rye and Winchelsea, fortified
against French
pirates who brought their boats up where the sea ran
now inland, Land Gate, Water Gate, names record
the old topography, a strategic importance

                    further, as the sea drew back
                    along the Rother's course, did it then
                    turn inland, westward, to drown seven parishes
                    of nine at Hastings

By the Queen's Head I stood plotting a course
along the dykes across the marsh to the facing slope
catching the afternoon sun
and sheltering me from the wind as I walked
along its contour to enter Rye
across the sluice
from the other side

Second Song in Spring

The small flowers sing
my songs for me

are stars as I
go through the fields

sniffing the Spring
air is balm to

my sense of the
country blossoms

at my feet, prim
-roses and violets

alder copse and trim
-med hazel thicket I

cross barbed wire
catches the lamb's wool

An Invocation: To Snow For

Cover this city, clothe it
let its people awake
to a day of white streets
a Sunday so you lie
undisturbed by employment

            Let it lie
the city, bride-like in white
before whatever visit it

            lie
on the pavements, first
to the feet of worshippers

            let it lie
this city by the Atlantic
– cold winds come

bearing your six-branched crystals
inland, let them fall
here, as I spell this

            fall
through the day, to maintain
your laying

            fall
thick, so that all
be covered

            fill the air
that it become a denser medium

            fill space
that our eyes be dazzled with vision

            fill our minds
that they be more than they were

before we slept
            we are to awake

The Daffodil on my Table

Streaks of yellow show through
the unfolding green spears
three buds about to open among
a cluster of pointed leaves
. more as the first
unfolded, blossomed, and died
new buds pushed through
the waxen leaves, yellow
emerging from green, unfolding
blossoming, dying, it went on
blooming for six weeks
in February and March 1963

The City Rises

The city rises between two rivers
East and West there is no view
to the other shore beyond
the wharves   nothing   yet
from over there it rises so
all view ends upon it
all is drawn to
its high buildings which might
serve as outlooks to westward
land and eastward sea
and are
only for the visitor to see
whence he has come
the citizen
looks up to them
beyond
only the sky

The Evening's Occupation

She works at her maths   patiently
the voice from the next room
explains when she cries
'I don't understand' giving
a running commentary 'Hey
65 into 13 is stupid'
before running in and the voice
subsides with hers to a murmur
of divides and carries and giving so
I can no longer make out the working
and the poem
                              takes its way
about the quiet apartment
cat and dog asleep, the lady
out waiting at table, her daughter
and my friend engrossed with her
numbers   I   with the poem

The Joke

About three quarters of an hour after she got to the bar she said she'd tell a joke; it was perhaps pertinent to the situation. It was about Hitler in his bunker at the end of the war and she assumed a German accent to say Mein Führer, Mein Führer, we are defeated, our forces are falling back on every front. She heard herself unable to carry off the accent, she could not tell the joke and so came to the point at once. Hitler leaned across the map of Europe that lay before him and looked at his generals, her eyes were hostile as she glared across the table demanding a response she grated All right then. No more Nice Guy!

She sat back still looking straight at him, her glare softened in satisfaction as she did not get the response she demanded. He was the third she'd told the joke who'd failed to see the point.

What was the point he wondered, how is it pertinent? He thought the situation included him. Later he remembered she'd said he was the third she'd told the joke and saw how much she felt it touched upon herself. Her voice rasped No more Nice Guy. He still did not see the point as she patiently explained that Hitler thought he had been playing it straight till then and now was going to do what he really felt like.

She would be true to herself, and was just finding out who that was. But need you feel such anger? he began she stopped him angrily Won't you understand anything? It's good for me to be angry if I am. The occasion isn't important.

He looked about her, trying to understand her anger and how it embraced everything as it was contingent upon her. Himself. He did not like to feel contingent. He walked about the city and felt uncomfortable. The life, he felt, was hard; a succession of tenement lodgings, people fed badly and dressed poorly, so many he met and knew, perhaps, three or four. She lived there year after year and it seemed that her perception of the world became the way it impinged upon her sense of herself. Yet she was hardly aware of how she touched others, and said so. She was in a world and hated it. 'For my own confusion, and for the world's, I blame the world' she had written him. Yet the world... She had none of her own even. So he looked on her.

She would not meet his gaze, and went to telephone her friend to see what she was doing that evening. She came back to the table and said her friend would meet her there in half an hour; they would probably go to the cinema together. He waited to say Hello to the wife of the man who was his closest friend in the city, and her irritation mounted as they sat without speaking. She began to tear her cigarette package and then spoke angrily to him This is the last time I'll ever see you to talk to. Her friend his friend's wife entered the bar and sat down without speaking to him. The three got up together to leave; there was snow on the pavement. At the corner he said Goodbye and turned down the cross street where he was staying. As he walked away he saw the joke at last and laughed.

Poem

the pink sky recedes

westward
     that will be

down the lake
       the sky's dome still
smoky blue
as blue

   rainclouds drive across
the lake
     &
eastward
dusk has fallen

in the west
the last pink fades
        behind
the facing roof

here only the heavens
show the land's lie

Some Other Occasion
Joan's

Goodbye Goodbye
I am coming back, Mother

standing on the dock
I am crying

to see you there
the ship drawing out

I am coming back
I am crying

almost
wondering

When shall I leave?

The American Valentine

        I look out from
blue eyes that change
behind closed eyes   to green
before my eyes
        when I walk out
        there are police everywhere
        and mothers spy from passing cars
        men, ah, what is their perception
        fathers shackled and lovers
        will not let me be
the girl who gives herself
up   whatever moment

Privy Business

for D.H. Lawrence

'breasts that swayed
and made him frightened
as she rubbed them'

it's the familiarity
a woman uses
handling herself

towelling her damp breasts
or stemming
her blood's flow

while we go about
such matters as
strange to them

Thor's Fishing Trip

Thor disguised as a youth
to take Hymir fishing

for the serpent beneath the sea
that circles the little earth

His speed deceived
the protesting giant

as he rowed far
beyond the fishing ground

and baited the worm
with an ox head;

the worm bit hard
Thor braced his legs

so he bust through the hull
to stand on the sea's bed

to raise the coiling worm
and return its glare

with his hammer raised
to smash its skull.

But the frightened giant
cut the line;

Thor heaved him overboard
and waded to the shore.

Does the serpent lie dead?
or alive.

-o0o-

Originally to be titled 'There are certain names', the following poem was written for Charles Olson while Crozier was at Buffalo and it had its occasion in the reorganisation of the old London boroughs under the Greater London Council. Crozier suggested in a note from early 1967 that '[this] landscape has the dimension of myth, and my ability here depended very much on my distance from the scene of the poem. Any faults of detail to be found are unimportant.'

-o0o-

There are Names

East along the river
towards the sea
the maritime boroughs
on the south bank

Deptford, where Peter lived
with the shipwrights he came to learn from;
the palace at Greenwich
with its park and naval college; and
at the limits of the old county
the royal dockyards at Woolwich, and later
its royal arsenal

Eltham has a palace too
a couple of houses older than Greenwich
and more rural
you couldn't get there by boat
not on a day trip anyway
tootling down to hear Mr Handel
in a barge from Westminster

and that's alright because
the riverfront and the common
and Shooter's Hill attract you
towards Woolwich, and both were
Kentish anyhow, though the valley
takes you more easily to Lewisham
which wasn't

but now we're to
call the whole lot Greenwich
Woolwich be a failing parish
with a hip bishop
and closed-down works
and the parish of Eltham
go back to being royal

A Poem of Men

The man I love
lies out there
the continent away
and soon I shall travel back
the way both came, separately,
almost the world away from him
listening
to the country nurse
telling the story
of her life
I can't guess at, even this close
and when I've gone it will be even more
beyond me, that new life he finds.

It is
new, another he cares for much
says, not like here in the dying West,
nor here at the Mid-West's eastern edge
the dwindling ex Queen of the Great Lakes
I came to
and will leave
to find no other men lovely
as he, in my country
no man's company to love
but my father's
I didn't know my lack
before I found

among such desolation
such generosity in men

who bring me to him
I will leave for

the restriction he tells, of
who should be his like.

The Rainbow

as I wrote that I saw the sunrise
an aurora flashing crimson behind a building
in the blue dawn
then the disc's rim itself, I saw it rise
above the roof's edge, the image on my retina
of steel cut with a blow torch;
the disc still rose, in four minutes
it was detached, crimson gone,
the whole sky lit with it
and my eye
dazzled, cannot see these words. I know
the earth whirling on its axis
against the direction of the sun
climbing so swift in the sky
already its heat on my brow
might be of bright noon, I feel
the morning
gone, eating breakfast at 6.30 a.m.

2

What I intended to write was how Ursula reminds me of my mother, an assistant teacher in that horrible grade school, waiting to go to college where she will learn botany. Those mean kids, like Colin B., I taught him, and now twice he's mentioned in her letters. Poor Ursula! At the beginning of my England at the end of the novel when she saw the collier suburbs advancing towards each other from three directions, three separate villages. They have all joined up now, and I live there. Earlier the way her Grandfather went drinking in the city pubs on Saturday night drove me to nostalgic frenzy. But it was really the way the children went by train into the city to school or work. Or in another book David Herbert leaving his mother so early each morning, to catch the train, one with carriages and compartments, not some interurban subway.

With Her New Lover

When I left I never thought
of coming back, how it would be
when you return
you are a stranger
to what has gone on

and what you have done
is nothing
to what you left
                    what you want

their change to you is greater

what you've become
what you were
to them

-o0o-

Crozier had sent the following poem to Prynne in April 1965 and it elicited a careful and lengthy reply which not only highlighted the qualities of the poem but also hinted at the way forward.

-o0o-

How Does It Go?

I want to write this poem while I still can
hold to that loveliness I know
fades easily

                    In the sun
the ice wrapping the branches
shone and sparkled as it melted
and slipped from its object.
The air was filled with its falling
tinkle and the hollow sound
that cracked and spread from my footfall
walking across a frozen field

to a seat in the sun, but a cold wind
blowing in my ear
from across the lake at my back
the University

I don't want to talk about that
cause to my presence here but of what's come
about since I have

been young love's

loveliness
I spoke of

and would sing
you now

young lov-
ers we

were once to
-gether sleep

-ing in one
bed togeth-

er lay in
arms unused

to others' charms

Song's failure
in its rhyme
to say what's meant
that lovely ice that girl
how to have both
in the poem?

In a night the trees are freed
the ice melts
into soggy ground soon
to put forth fresh herbage
and spring flowers

the trees to put forth leaves too
where birds sing in the sky
shining through bare branches

as the season changes you
could make your life
in allegory

but I cannot
cast what will be to that
form of nature
will fit any story
I make up, it can't be helped
nature, can't help me

unless I sing

all loveliness
this day

's this girl's

this man's in

every season
every land

-o0o-

Prynne wrote in his letter to Crozier (17 April 1965, Cambridge):

Your poem I have just read, for the first time, so that I'll feel my way into a brief comment. Trivially, there's a catch at 'footfall' which I can't take as literal force nor (otherwise) as wry & so on. Duncan does it, too easily for me, I would want a purer sense of word, at least for its place (thus, 'herbage' is fine, since you elide *rhythmically* into that kind of allusion). What strikes me about the piece more generally is that the schism you speak of is very nearly held across. Not entirely, at such short notice; but there is a shape which is workable. The nub is crucially in 'this day / 's' and the arrival which this brings off. So we come to it as the allegory you've spoken of, the adverbial phrase full of grammar and other people's language, which across that vacant line is swivelled to be a vessel for loveliness. It contains the sound of it, so that you can (by apposition) set down its landscape, and the two figures can become, exactly, what explicitly you tie it up to be. This isn't rime (or even rhyme), which is an obvious backdoor by which to get frost into the technical format, since that can only work by illicit identity: in unimportant respects these are similar, and so 'therefore' in much more important respects they are workably the same. That's a tired way of being carried to what it'd be nice to say, and something of a trick. Maybe the other's a piece of virtuosity as well, but there's a wrist to it the first can't now have, a turn in the elements we do have, now, about us. Also, the contraction of the line, which had previously set a pretty (staccato for disguise) song against the European meditative length of statement, is also broken or set off, so that stanzaic rhyme is out as well (as in pun by contour at the left hand margin). 'Song's failure' &c (that block) is too short to be the same kind of enquiry, though just longer than the hyphenated song, and is followed by rich Petrarchan imminence of amorous emblem in the long line. Such strategy gives excellent point to setting 'allegory' into its own icefloe, and releasing the old question through a concessive afterthought.

'Not entirely' I say at this point, still only half-knowing the workings, maybe because you've let more into it. The good humour with which you come at it slips in an occasional coyness, not protective but perhaps over-willingly friendly nonetheless. I refer to a link demanding maximal tact: 'what's come / about since I have / been / ...' The position of 'been' is critical, could be to hold it from doing too much too quickly, a holding off that's not so honest as what follows. The pastoral play is warm and also nipping, but even there also there's a difficulty in saying it out clearly that provokes the dalliance with the renaissance pop singer's rhyme. This latter is a difficulty which is part of the narrative, and maybe the uncertainty of 'been' held over the void is part of how to join without fictive rhyme. But 'been' (as example, say) I can't feel as completely contained, as also I can't the idiom which produces 'cause' (mainly, since it might, but needn't, be a contraction for because). It might take you further than the provisional honesty of 'what's *meant*'. Up to this, though, I like it very well, and can see that the narrative of it could have very significant consequences for what else you write. Quite an unprecedented form of syllable.

In July 1967 Prynne wrote to Crozier referring to having received the recently published volume:

> Thank you for the book, I was quite invaded on reading it, as something now bound together, by the sense of your title. Of course you could hardly linger with that self staring from the cover & no less insistently from most of the other pages. But if we are separated by distinctions of category from what we wish for, that doesn't diminish the force of an unidentified but pervasive sense of desire.
>
> What will happen now I wonder, since such an arbitrary terminus sets its term also on what may be to come.

II
ESSEX AND KEELE

Crozier was extremely busy when he started at the University of Essex in the autumn of 1965. Not only had he already set up his own press, Ferry Press, a year earlier, but also he now began the Wivenhoe Park Review *at Essex, co-edited by Tom Clark. Both of these ventures were an expression of Crozier's high regard for what was happening in America. The earliest volumes to appear from Ferry Press were underwritten by the subscriptions of a few dozen interested individuals and the first book was a prose piece,* Thread, *by the Black Mountain artist and writer Fielding Dawson. This was followed soon afterwards by two volumes of poetry by the Boston writer Stephen Jonas, as well as by work by John James, Jeremy Prynne, Peter Riley, Douglas Oliver, John Temple and Chris Torrance. The importance of Ferry Press in establishing new voices in England was long-lasting, and its significance continued as it became merged with Jean Crozier's own Silver Hounds Press. With the* Wivenhoe Park Review *Crozier placed into even sharper relief the influential importance of American poetry. The first issue contained work by Olson, Dorn, Jack Spicer and John Wieners, as well as the first publication of a series of poems by Prynne that were to be later collected in* The White Stones. *Unlike the carefully designed and printed books from Ferry Press, the first issue of* Wivenhoe *was a hurried affair:*

> Tom Clark & I started Wivenhoe Park Review when we went to Essex in 1965. Initially this was to be with the university's patronage: I think copy for the first issue was typed in the English department, & it may even have been printed in house. In any event it was a disaster, inadequately perfect bound because the cover didn't include a spine, and copies quickly disintegrated.
>
> (letter from Crozier to Ian Brinton, 12 September 2006)

In January 1966 Crozier began editing The English Intelligencer, *which ran until 1968, as well as extending the range of his own work with poems that were to be published in his next volume,* Walking on Grass. *Thirty-six issues of* The English Intelligencer *were published between January 1966 and April 1968 – roughly one every three weeks – and it was circulated by mailing list to a varying number of English poets (ranging from 25 to 65 names at different times). There was always a hard core of a dozen or so and these were the poets who gave the magazine its consistency. This intensity of activity was in itself an important fact of English poetry in the 1960s, since this core of contributor-readers included many of the most active and interesting younger English poets, whose work continued to develop and who found the regular correspondence of ideas and presentation an important part of the growth of their own poetic consciousness. The magazine was originally conceived as an attempt to draw together various English poets whose work was thought of as avant garde and who were strongly aware of contemporary American influences. The poets included those who were variously associated with other magazines of the time, such as* Migrant, the Resuscitator, Prospect, *and* Outburst, *as well as more isolated individuals such as Lee Harwood, Jim Burns and Tom Pickard;* The English Intelligencer *provided these poets with a common meeting-place. There was no initial editorial line beyond the selection of poets to whom to circulate the sheets of the magazine. Since Crozier was involved in editing the first issue of* Wivenhoe Park Review *he became aware of the peculiarly 'English' project of the* Intelligencer, *and was concerned to produce this second magazine with an entirely different character to the trans-Atlantic Essex University journal. The free availability of a mimeograph machine gave him the means to do this, and it is quite feasible to see the* Intelligencer *as part of the inspiration for Tom Clark's* Once *series of magazines: both were produced on the same mimeograph machine and were closely similar in format. In a note dated July 1969 Crozier commented on the history of the* Intelligencer*:*

> The function of the Intelligencer as it had been originally conceived was never realised; its real achievement on the other hand is still in the process of fruition. The magazine was actually run-down and brought to a halt between December 1967 and April 1968 when it became apparent that a) the size of its readership had become unwieldy, b) it had various levels of readership involvement, and c) those most closely involved felt that the pattern of exchange that had been established had become stultifying.

The relationship between The English Intelligencer *and the development of Crozier's own poetry can perhaps be best traced in the two letters sent to him by Prynne in 1966, both of which commented on the poems that would go to make up the collection* From the Root. *Dating from 1966–7, some of these poems were published in the* Intelligencer *before being included in* Walking on Grass *(Ferry Press, 1969).*

In his first letter, Prynne wrote:

…I did very specifically like the Two Loves even though in some ways I can see it's easy to do. And I would guess that I know why the other long piece is important, since as I read it you are trying to slide without breaking anything back into the continuity of this side of the Atlantic. There *is* that rational introspection about mode which, having been trained to, we must be careful in setting down: I know that, you may be sure. It was there in the Roof poem as well and I do respect that, since in a tighter social conspiracy it looks bourgeois and may for all I know even be so. The domestic is not in violation of the preferred forms of knowledge, and so, here, it will have to supersede them. I think that's as you say quite wildly hard and as yet is quite unknown, almost. Thus, I am proud of the delicacy & adjustment of our touch with the past and will in no sense buy any of that moan about Europe's fabled shore etc. It's no polemical fact that there is *no* threat we may not envisage, if the forms are discreetly exercised. I don't expect such a matter to be interesting, though: just so long as the drab stain isn't there as well. The cast of it in my case is to get into something else – i.e., not society which is doomed but the community of uncertain lovers. And don't take that as wild because I am very sane in this question of who we really are, accurate as a needle, I know quite enough about the supposed banality of Sunday morning & the radio on for lunch. Given that problem I would go for purity, in the most strictly ethical sense, fairly like the architect: something provisional but we are so rich we will die of gout & affection if we don't move, we must learn to float & to love the water, to disclose the knowledge we needn't even *ask* for. All right, I know what you're doing you may be sure, & I admire it as well (sometimes to a quite extraordinary extent). The time will come and pour down like a libation, it will flow like oil into the ground.

(J.H. Prynne, letter to Crozier, 2 March 1966, Cambridge)

The second letter, dated 13 September 1966, was published in the Intelligencer, *an open document recording some thoughts about these recent poems of Crozier's*:

Thanks for sending the poems. The apple poem needs no direct comment, but I think I do have some feeling about the others which I simply note. It has to do, I think, with the pathos of distance, which you take on rather too often I would say. This gives you a rich vein of sentiment and even those delicious gestures, just the suggestion of a catch in the voice, but at the same time an intensely *literary* option on whether to pursue it or not, as a figure in one of Puttenham's counterfait modes. Now pathos and even poverty may truly be one of our present conditions, but the flower on the bush is a glide into poignant suggestion, which is not pathos at all but a kind of court device: 'Or is it not perchance more requisite our courtly Poet do dissemble not onely his countenances & conceits, but also all his ordinary actions of behaviour, or the most part of them, whereby the better to winne his purposes & good advantages, as now & then to have a iorney or sicknesse in his sleeve?'

Even if it's a fantasy, the sequel is a painful separation of assertions which now at this time ought especially to be kept close. Astrophil in the mirror *is* a Figure of Fortune, and his lament was properly both fluent and gilded. But here the movement of the lines is *removal*, poetic licence in the other sense of 'sweet'. Nor even hermaphrodite, the moon shines over like some argent coverlet. Where is the true metal in all this, and sorrow proud to be advanced so. You must begin to know what I mean, Andrew, this piece like *nowhere to fly to* earlier, is so discreet as to be painfully *dull*. We do know that sentiment has to do with touch, is intimate as well as public, that the language too has its pulse and can be moved 'delicately' (another Shakespearian pun). And I'm not advancing any case for mortification, but you are so much the opportunist, which casual & discreet ornament you then claim for some urgency of form: *O sweetness*.

It's also technical. The words are easy because also light. The occasional promise of event is just a spread over your abstract nouns: tenderness, bar, difference, *what*. I might even refer to a continuing hint of derision towards the subject – the very exposure of it a kind of priggish excitement to the reader. If a set of language is to need and deserve confidence it must keep its own kind of fidelity: it must be true to its purpose. And what is *I sit alone at my window*. True to an occasion, you try not to be at all artificial, but *nowhere* true to any degree of purpose. My argument is in some kind of vice here, because the purpose is of course the retrospective formalism of the occasion. Your nostalgia is very artful, the reader is left carrying about the abandoned tones of this world. It's accomplished, and for a lutenist that would maybe draw the whole listener back into play.

But not any more: our ambiguities now are *quite* different, and have little connection with the *authentic*. The scales have been repeatedly forced. I don't know how the true ease would sound, but we can't go back to hurt as a refinement of nonchalance, with all the elisions of sweetness put against an impartial notion of the public art. Your language is no more than arch inasmuch as it invokes those assumptions – that's no longer a rack on which anyone is stretched. As a way of life it's even more uninteresting. What *is* the difference, and how *does* it then set (as you passingly refer to it)? In one degree at least, the private purity of a life held entirely by occasion *sacrificed* to the 'exigencies' of the public conspiracy (called *world*). So that the heart is again a walled garden, only this time this is not allegory but exile – you never *live* there, on any terms except sufferance. Thus pathos in this mode is actually another wedge between those transposed conditions (trust, desire, the open window) and the world intactly grabbed back into the silver forest: the very oldest idea of 'nature' (causing the wild bees to swarm & produce *honey* as well as *eloquence*).

It's easy to be dissatisfied with this poem, easier to feel absurd for taking it as more than a shifted dalliance. But I do think it inflicts on our shared language a shine it cannot use, and that you ought to be doing something else. Is that unfair?

-o0o-

Walking on Grass

FROM THE ROOT

At Least I've A Roof Over My Head

Thin sounds of rain are in the air
outside   does that matter?
it can't rain in here, though it does
over the space where I am sitting
the roof carries it away and I
am kept dry and know it only
in those thin sounds

they have since stopped   occasionally
the sound of a motor passes
on the bypass with an imagined
hiss of scattered moisture in the distance

a distant light confounds with a spot
of yellow paint on the window   but for
the passing and repassing of lilac twigs
blown in the silent wind

even further the oscillation of an electric train
overtaken by the sound of poplars
in the sudden wind

another car, another train, the sounds
hiss and sway across to
me   the eyes focus and refocus
to bring it all in

to a place beneath a roof because of
which I am here to be a centre
to what I can't help but be
centre to   it would be
the same   in any direction

Three Night Pieces

The cat visits me and mews
in the night I prepare for bed
she looks where I stand and think
this as I take pen and pad
she jumps to the bed I sit upon
purrs and treads the dishevelled bedclothes
nudges the moving pen to smudge
'I' and 'take' and settle
beside me with regular purr and paws
tucked in front, her tail beneath.
I'm not interesting any more.
I am, and put away my pen to move
her to sleep

The dead cigar poisons the mouth
that draws on it
the ash flakes   onto the sheet
and isn't noticed   a lighted
window looks onto this   and between

them the darkness fills a gap
until the sun lets the trees back

Sleep fills my head, my eyelids droop
my fist is heavy around my pen

if I am still I hear the voices in my head

each effort to forward this silences them

Ways With Dice

1 If we took each other in hand.
I don't know if I am serious enough
to write it as a poem.
I doubt yet that I could. This at any rate
is a first throw. Cup in hand
I enter the game, throwing, throwing.
Never able to work out odds
on or evens: is this to gamble?

2 If I extend you my hand
would you take it? If I'd said
will you I would already be dealing
direct. You're not here. Neither am I almost.
The next time I extend my hand will be to switch off
the alarm clock.
It will be nearly six o'clock. There will be time
to reflect further upon the problem of hands.

3 Images can't be got away with
or from. Isn't the head
a bigger gamble than hands?
No, I said the head is more important
than his hands to the gambler in my head.
They keep coming, but I won't hide.
If I stick it out I'll get to what I want
to say, my head told me. My heart belied
that hope. 'Come to bed' it said 'Before
it is too late.'

4 A hand holds a cup
as another hand. A hand shakes
a cup almost as a hand.
Perhaps this hand will cast
a lucky number. Please,
don't let it be empty.

(Note: A hand is better turned
to turn up trumps. This is consonant
with gaming, but not dicing, let us say.)

5 A hand is also of cards.
My cup runneth over. In my hand
with tea probably, a good drink
with or without
milk, sugar, lemon, etc.

6 The intention of a poem like an acorn
grows into a great big tree that looks
as though it's in the way. Molecular biology
pursues this analogy
and kills it. That is a long way
from hands, cups, cards, and gambling
men, but look where they've got me.

(Note: In line 2 the terminal demonstrates
an inert metaphor of vision. I may not look
as though I'm looking where I'm going but I am
getting there.)

7 Here is the cup, please hold it.
It is my hand bent to hold yours.
If you like you can shake it but if
you let go carelessly the die might fall
and roll into a dark corner and
never find us again. This is the die.
I don't know any more about it
but that.

(Note: The die obviously means something
even if it's not meant to. There is the voice
it adopts. It is a self-important die
that invites.)

8 With twelve edges, each common
to two faces, and twelve divided
by two, the die has
six faces numbered with black dots.
The poet dealing in proportion
works out mathematical formulae, which isn't
anything new.

(Note: The poem's qualification
of the poet's profession
to have written this poem:
it was the habit of a lifetime.)

Towards

As the sun sets in the west it is brighter there
the northern sky lighter
while the river drawn back
by the tide in the darkening sea
to it flows out of that fading
western and midland brightness
south of the white buildings
of the tiring commerce that placed them there
they slide into the night. The south is black
and it is markets and warehouses and railway track
I cross the bridge to. Ridden in
from the eastern counties with the falling sun
infusing my eyes with sleep for the lids droop
to curtain the glare and the train cradles asleep

Marriage

All those domestic interiors
I've ever entered, with husband and wife
proudly inhabited by their things:
high, spacious, airy, they are rooms
and in them such gorgeous furniture
of such declaratory origin
chosen with loving care.
Love and care, that's what I feel for these friends
I end engrossed in the trappings of.

It's like the Sunday papers, worse
it's like snowed-up Buffalo, where everyone is married
with perhaps more children, and the shops to furnish them
emblems, the proper preserve of the poor.
Maybe those people are just provincial. Or not poor
in spirit. Does that mean my friends are poor
in spirit?

I want to go out
to a pub, or for a walk in the park
with a friend who's deserted his wife.
I don't want to be invited back for coffee
if your wife won't be pleased, because I am, too,
considerate of me. If she wanted to see me
maybe she would have come out too,
or even have been there instead of you.

So don't talk to me on gala night
when you're out with your wife and everyone else is
because she will be bored and you
embarrassed, by the high joy of being on your own.

The Kitchen

The moon is circled but not to be seen
in this room. Jonathan King has gone to the moon
he sings and it has no more to do with this room
than any other he is beamed into. So we are purged
and have what is still here though the tune changes

and everyone hears something different of love and
happiness. Here they're the dark brown tea I drink
in the blue and white cup I have handled for months
in water, through damp linen, lifted through air,
at my lips, cracked and stained. The stove
crackles and hisses full of coke, more like the
crushing of egg shell than the clatter of a tin
saucer of milk on the tiles in the next room
as the cat laps it dry. You know I'm here
in the room too, but you're not, you're listening
in another room which will fit you as familiar
as this room me. I've said I love you and you
have kindly listened, and now? We need some satisfying
conclusion. For you to be a room to me is neat
but unseemly. Later perhaps I will find it, or you
will for me. In our lives I've found the poem goes on
as long as another problem.

Sweet Words on Honeyed Lips

Can I go on to wound myself
on your indifference
who hold me in despite in all
but words? Those words are sweet
and stern and speak of loving
even as you turn and take your presence
from me. You love the back that's turned
and moves away, yours or another's,
retreating from what love was said about.
What's left but sediment, the lees of talked of
feeling, to cloud up in my mind
as I grope there to explore what's
happened. Too many careful words
describe the passion we know so well
we want to feel, and what's happened
is felt as so much worse, or tragic, later
when the chosen words of hope and intent
we loved to speak prove false and but for them
no-one would feel deceived.

Nowhere to Fly To

Let us not take our sweetest dreams
for the contour of our present life
which is dearer to me.
A house in the country, a river, a competence
of riches, to be spoken for
but not inhabited. As I thought I would disengage
from the corporation of money, for my own virtue
though not purity, before I recalled
the numbers, the depressed areas, there
already. The outside has failed
not us but in itself. I want the inside
to know it and not be tainted. The workings
are not the whole, and poor men
are still to be found who embarrass the places that stride
onward, as King Hill Hostel, West Malling, Kent.
The rich South East! Yes, to escape it
into the desolate North, the spaces
the wind keeps fresh as it blows
the stench of Rowntrees over half York.
But beyond, the moors, where the true man
can live, buy his castle, I never saw so much money
till I came here he couldn't help but exclaim
driving past the sweet preserve village greens.
The preservation of rural England, the seduction
to anger in the picture of a water mill burnt
for a film prop. It is the picture we love
half the time, and I love
my anger, and dream my cockeyed dreams.
Rather stay where you are, and be contained
in all the motions you take, that holds
all possibility. Inside out
side it bears down equally, and if our part
brings no return we're in it and ground down
the same, but fail to see it happen.
Where it flourishes, I'll grow.

A Day, a Garden, Stay Awake to Dream

I was tired and lass-
itude lay over me as I
lay on my bed. What got me up
and to the table
was to write this. Enough
to get me to my feet, to sit here
with damp hair and wanting to go to sleep.
I have done nothing today
(there's euphemism) but arrange for a job
I begin tomorrow, and on my way home
look at some tropical plants and smell
the delight of liquid fertiliser. In a dull narration
I feel dull, and passed my hand over my face
as I noticed reflected in the window.
There the lilac blooms
stand out of the darkness, I tell their colour
and from it the green of leaves. The mass moves
in the wind, and is the opposite of dense.
I never found a word for that. It moves
as in a denser medium, as to the incoming tide
the anemone unfurls and sways.
The lilac's sweetness
doesn't penetrate, yet by night
the tobacco plant blooms sweetest. I am awakening
to this green life, infer, and find
a hand across my eyes and a chill strike
across my shoulders and constrict my sides.
It's panic. My dreams have been
of torture and rejection, and I awoke sweating
wondering at the source of the finished image.
What can I know of torture? Then tonight I watched
Americans practising on each other
in a TV picture. It was formal, but I think
of an informal daily torture. A man screamed
in the street drunk on meths and it crept
cold beneath my skin. To one another
we are cold and it is metaphor
as it is physiology and I am
afraid. A body's touch
is warmth

and I am not afraid
afterwards

The Harp

An open book : work. *This metre*
which in England outlived the Anglo-
Saxon language several centuries.
These are only years. The tree is growing
it renews its leaves, they fall.
A thought transcribed over a century
is ink still damp upon the paper.
Wind moves in the leaves, rain gleams
upon them. It makes them make a
sound like rain drops falling, they move
against each other. Wind and rain
in silence touching sounds out of the earth.

Now Evening, Last Night and Tonight

The future never comes, in the sense
that it's not what we might enjoy now,
and is only sacrificed, in the gesture of walking out
on the present moment. Change it, including you,
or you were never there, and when tomorrow comes
as you imagined it, you find today
nothing is changed and you're still made unhappy.
And when you say, I want to be
Happy, I should think of Keats not looking for *Happiness*
if it be not in the present hour,
the sun and a sparrow, going down
in the west, and chirping in the lilac boughs
for evening: the cat knows them, sprawled
on a tarpaper roof in the declining rays.

A Small Orchard

1

A world   is apple trees
of global fruit

to entrance the eye
with fullness

in gardens
full

of trees   in leaves

briefly
replete

as the eye

was : knew
everything

as content

in apples
just   this year's

in all
the world's

a lovely apple

2

A world   in an apple tree

eyecatching globules
stuffed

into the gardens
almost   they're so

expansive

quite hide
the gorgeous foliage

big as your eyes
grow   you couldn't stomach

all that goodness

gone to seed
in fact

they'll grow
as well

in all the world

is lovely
apples

3

Picture the apples on the tree

glimpsed past laburnum, plum, and lilac
hard against a barren pear
the smallest   only

bearing fruit

is

worldy bright

green
fairer than leaves
they're nestled in
the apples

draw the eye
the same   another day

to set the hand to capture
the fruit droop
from the bough
on a bank of leafage

at her bole
a roof curved

over my head
the sky

starry with apples

Stay On and What Is Lost

A girl's voice singing *Summertime*
upon the air, somewhere close, another,
older, serves behind the bar

that apart
                we are all men
within, is pleasing, and a smile
plays over every lip, a glass
at every hand, stands, frothy
the smiling mouths, wiped
and replenished.
                Five men in middle
and old age
talk about the weather, their holidays
each speaks and everybody laughs.
Another two throw darts
don't talk, each takes his turn
and chalks his score, the other
pulls the darts and waits
till the board is clear. Two more
come in and stand
their backs against the bar as one
displays a complicated motion.
The five men leave
the bar is spacious. Next door the song
has changed to an old

male voice   *Del Shannon*
singing   *Runaway.*   Sure
summer's gone, but who need run
this autumn, from what is found here.

Sprung from the Root

No point but in strength, to be any
where but at that definition
as endurance, not merely suffering
but not faltering
from the past, that is also
definition, like a deceptive passiveness
that turns to action which the first term
makes power, and force
is what strength contains, turned out
wards, lining such shapes of love
for it to recognise
its own, in the dancing point, say
          rose bloom in the air
          upon the flower, oh slacken
          the pace, and the heart
          beat slower, as words come

Tired, Dies

Dreaming again, it's not what any of us thought:
nowhere for the eye to rest but in the socket
where it rolls around, scans everything
sees nothing, resting there.
It would roll up in sleep behind closed lids
but a glaze there still shimmers on the brain
and the eyelids tremble with the light

and gape again. Somewhere behind them aches
or maybe they. The lids pull close
and the scene is focussed in the confine
to children exercising against a green field.
Like that the eyes slide, sideways in panoramic
green ribbon of white moving shapes
or rise to a grey sky hazed through dark lashes;
all's in, on the mind, and lies flat.

Out of the Deep

Here I always think of the sea
its heavy surge at night
makes much noise as heavy traffic
there isn't here   sometimes
in the background. Or I hear its waters
tug back over the shingle
and a hush before they pour
back in a wave that scours stone up over stone
in one roar   at this distance
when the wind is different, or the tide
not at some point where its noise is all one
as it pours across the beach it is always
shaping   to make new sounds.
Nothing can plot them. Trite they are
always the same
and fill the night each time I am in earshot.

Follow, Shadow

How long these buds take
to come fully into leaf. Unclenched like this
they've been for more than a week
but not spreading
out to turn green in the sun.
Aren't they pale, in this dark
like flowers on the forsythia
growing by them, but inverted.

Flecks. They have been awaited,
left, anxiously, and returned to
in time, they take their time.
Mark time. Coarse, flat, and green,
turned to the sun, and showing how it's gone.

For Amity

What remains of a visit
to Wicken Fen
a cardboard strawberry punnet
turned upside down
by Amity

        coloured in
red   &
rows of three
hearts along each side
drawn in lead pencil

stuck into the base
a plastic cocktail-stick
over all raises a green
        heart : *Dear*
                    Andrew
              I wish you
              did not
              have to go.
              Love
                    Amity.
inscribed upon

        a paper   placed within
pasted in a notebook
retains the memory

        like Jefferson
in this picture too
bigger than his sister and three years younger
wrestling in the back of the camper
subduing him

her smile breaks up into her freckles
the smell of strawberries getting everywhere
            sweet

heart, whose name does not
belie her, to be thanked for
herself

Seaside Fragments

1

Not been used for so long
there's no chalk for the shove hapenny table
and no game for us.
I will steal some, or maybe the landlady
will buy. She wishes we would come and play
more often.

Mrs. Johnson it is *invites*
us, it is her trade
card, *to sit in the sun*
of course   at the Sun Inn
and the pun can't be passed up. It shines
from their faces too. As my grandfather's sign
he painted shone over them all
when they took this photo, from before
her time   ten years back
twenty away from me. Wrapped up
like his skittles and building bricks
gathering dust in the attic, it went
the way of all things. I need this picture
to recall it and feel sad
or sometimes outrage. Even the landlady
doesn't like the replacement as much.
Sitting outside the Sun isn't the same
I tell someone, who takes my word
This town must have some power for me?
No, I say, easing us both
past some sincere difficulty
but it's so nice here
in the early morning, been light

for some time, sun
already on the houses across the valley
swallows lashing up and down between.
Two cats with the garden
to themselves, and sparrows astir
in the rafters. It is composed
and changes.

2

So I could stop like that
submit to other preoccupations
just getting up in the morning.

Two hours work a day
so I'm not tired enough to want an earlier bedtime
soon takes it out of you. Many will be at work
while I take an afternoon nap.
But that's what this town is like.
The beach covered in greasy bodies
keeping the place going with their currency,
local talent slumps, the boys get giddy
mounting a short-term inflationary spiral.
Two hours a day spent
part of this great enterprise
tapping all Europe. I wonder
would my grandfather be ashamed
for me   and just wonder.

But why should he? Tressell showed his workingmen
the keystone of the system.
No honour in being exploited.

No ethic in work.

Another morning with seagulls
and I suppose a thrush
time to go to bed
time to get up
no work today

that's better
phone my uncle later
'Please come to the Yorkshire Grey
And teach us to play snooker.'

Two Poems

I

Not here but not here
I think of you more than I thought
to. That is every day
I think of you some more
as well as I did yesterday.
It all mounts up
and I think about that. And think of you
as I do, a new thought
to add to the old
I wouldn't have had without you going.
I think about me and find you
thinking about me, together
in one thought, I recognise
and cry 'At last!' to you.
            Just a moment. Just
a thought turning
into two others
me, thinking, you,
should be here, as
you are
in my thoughts.

II

A lot of small words together
to hold back that impending darkness
or we are overwhelmed
alone. I is one word or
I am are two at other times.
These changes become us
as we might regain what we were.
I believe nothing to be lost.

As those same small words
sustained me till I could complete my thought
and are not of it. They disperse
to their original matter, our history,
clustered in you as well as me.
They are what's left, and not what's written,
I couldn't hold them down to that.
Nor can I write of you, how I would like to
know
you as you
are, I suppose
in a strange room, in a strange
town, on unfamiliar streets
your ordinary thoughts
hurt most, as I imagine them
knowing I can't be right. How you
are like me
doing something different
in the dark, nothing but words between us.

Out of Slumber

Not that its movement
turns us to the sun
to follow a fiery course
veiled in cloud

from eastern dawning
to western going down
into sleep
waves lap my eyelids
and upon my head
ocean closes

rocked in her bosom
breath moves easily
upon me, through me
soothed to bow my head
and shrink

into the earth
rolling in darkness
under me
lie quietly
carried along
our upper parts float

in the medium
flexed and relaxed
drawing strength
out of earth
to recreate

the Earth
a course stretching
from our feet
is lit as I
uncoil and lift

in the first long
horizontal ray

WALKING ON GRASS

Curtain

The curtain hung. It was looked at. It was
hung. It was stood back from
to be looked at. It stood out from
a black background. The stars were there
in the distance. Of space. It was
deep. On its surface the curtain
floated. Motionless. No air current
disturbed its folds. As it floated
away.

Love Poem

The trees on the hillside, forked and bare,
silhouetted in the night, and the noise the wind made
blowing in my ears, the need for your warmth
and the remote thought of moist unshaven armpits
accompanied me as I walked to the bus
and remain with me, back in my room.
The wind sounds in the chimney, something,
like shots being fired, is a canvas slapping.
And then it ripples. And you are far away
as ever you were last night, it stretches
my mind down the night-time roads
we drove along, which still lie there
though our wheels are not turning over them.
Just as they lay last night, while I
was drinking Nescafé reading James's *Portrait
of a Lady*, not thinking of you
as 150 miles of tarmacadam, but a voice
down a wire which broke down
outside Euston then started again, to
limp home, and tell me about it.

Fan Heater

It blows out air, with a
fan, which hums, it heats up
the air in its resistant
electrical coils, it takes it in
cold, through a vent in its top,
and blows it out hot
or cold as desired, with a choice
of three settings on its white control
knob – 2 kilowatts, or 1, or
cold – two red dots, one red dot, a
grey circle, and a grey dot showing
'off', and then it has a red light
to show the current's still going through it
somewhere, till it is unplugged or switched off
at the point. It is a pattern
of human cunning and sits there

like a black box blowing out
hot air through its handsome white enamel
finish grille.

In Daylight

Caught in the light
that spilled about you
you brushed colour on your lids
intent on your reflection
shoulders bent forward, behind you
in the larger mirror the brightness
of the sky held you
in silhouette & more real
than your back was to me

a cloud went past, and some birds
were singing, you rose
and turned to me, I rose
from the bed, to my arms,
you are so beautiful
            and held there.

Alarm

This one is pink, with a
black face, and hands and
numbers that glow in the dark
in soft green. Someone left it
in running order, it ticked away
at the first turn of the key.

I grow older, the beard sprouts
on my cheeks, another night
has fallen – time passes
say these hands

as they revolve, irregularly crossing,
till a mechanism is released
and a bell rings. And would stop
in its own time, as the main spring
would run down. To be
as someone left it, wanting
its own small attentions
to be real.

Stepping, into her Dream

The eyes are closed dark and the dark
hair frames them   dark lids
and the sound of life   deeply breathing
my sleeping love's head rests on the pillow
that frames her face

                              She is dreaming
she is waiting and from her waiting
rises   with a smile to her lover's face
again above her where his eyes
are drawn and his feet have
followed   to bend and join
her smiling   with a kiss

Natural History

Rain on the roof, in April
the slates resound to it, drumming
over those indoors

two starlings persist
and have the lawn to themselves
they strut about as usual
and make their own small rain squalls
shaking their feathers out

in snow succeeding to the rain
bird tracks around and converging
upon a piece of bacon fat
are making something clear
sparrows among these now
that the rain's stopped drumming
have cries that are audible among the silent starlings

the snow's worn clear through
to the grass under all this traffic
while the piece of fat still lasts out
and the snow in April nevertheless is falling

Mirror Mirror

All the faces that looked and failed
to be held there for ever or
what did they seek? What there is
in the background doesn't count, never
did: does Nature make herself

a mirror? before we started with language
to see ourselves quoted by her
in all her moods. And hold another
before her face, to make her
different, and somehow better

like us. The stream crystalline,
like glass, the green flags parched
and forgotten, as it hangs
upon the wall. So air is glassy
too, the recession of space upon

a wall our picture window making
outside into a discrete home movie,
looking at ourselves. So nice to see
our image upon the wall as pretty
as pictures as though we knew exactly

what to recognise and like
our souls' likeness

claim and say that
we inhabit what is still
stretching, beyond our grasp.

The Interference

Across a landscape cuts the transverse light
in an oblique glass windscreen
constant and frame of vision
                    eyesight casts upon it
and through to the road that carries on
a spate of signals

                              green to yellow,
slowing down, a shaft of light wipes
over the smeared glass
turning a corner into the sun

straight ahead due west
roseate imprinted inches in front
where the spots are dancing like Mayflies
smashed upon the pane
in a wild glow of sunset

          flickers   slides   forward   darts
recedes   what has been changing
and what holds the changes, there,
in an instant of confusion
closer to death
            the lights were red
or in the sky, a red ball over the horizon

making towards it, across just one
of a whole system of planets
stars sparkle near and far
the glass shines somewhere in between
with its own darkness

                         a window closed
against the colder air, drops falling
speckle glinting off the surface they're

borne forward on

                    wiped away
the lights all disappear in auras
scintillating up and across
to slide off overhead

                                        the sky is
black or blue, not clear, about their glitter
leading to a point that vanishes
they start from in a drawn perspective
where a town ends at a different darkness
that touches against the skin

Things stand out
in the beam of the headlamps, step back
into a darkness they occupied
as obstacles to avoid in an empty space
the lights search
                    for the body in motion
to force on into

                    the limits of anticipation
met in the perfect beam of a car
turning a corner drawn across the darkness
to break over the screen and abolish
everything beyond the sensation of sight

Yellow

Nature is penetrating, as the spirit moves
the yellow chair left out in the rain
slowly warps and stands unsteadily on three legs
its art desolate, not sat
but stood upon, the paint all scarred
and worn. Like a new growth
the wood has swollen in the joints and
the turned lines bend out of true.
Not a chair, no human subject
if it's left much longer. Beyond words
to describe it – a bit of colour

caught beyond a mass of leaves like
a purer element still arbitrary
where it has returned to an older place.

A Set of Nashe

Ease of feeling a new overcoat settle onto your shoulders
before stepping out into a virgin snow-field that's about
to be ploughed by nervous feet setting out for the shops
before they close to get something for a quiet supper
for two or three crabs or quail or some strawberry ice-
cream from tins to be seasonal and greet the feeling of chill
with those slender wrists as they slide out at the ends of the
expensive sleeves and then slipping into the woollen mittens
detect a distinct savour of woodsmoke on the evening breeze
as the leaves burn nostalgically in the park waiting
to return to the kind of protean substance they came from
just shortly before when the season fell after the holiday
you're now remembering and wishing they'd not fallen as you
do.

Diary

Underneath the sky it's clear we're
both standing on bits of ground that are
continuous with each other. We're reflected
up there like Gemini which is reassuring
if you think of it – all that calm eternity.
I mean despite all that rolling around annually,
coming and going, they don't really change
at all, you can think about them
the same this month, next year
and the year after that, it doesn't make any difference
not to the way you feel, unless you want
to think about that too. So although the sky's
gone all dark (night) and the window has

misted over (winter) and the room smells
of paraffin fumes (cold) so that
'sky' is almost only an idea you have when
you're doing something else, it still is
'the sky' like it is when you go out
in the morning 'to work' & it reassures you
that can't last forever, because it's reminding you
of the appointment you have to keep this Thursday at 10.

To John James

Every time you see him John's fringe has grown shorter
so he waves it at you, and with the steel-framed
sartorial spectacle of an illustrious trans
tight vested poet, and a pleated vent,
he's on home ground. Byronic elogence of silent
praises stems like an auracle from his flair-
ing nostrils. He likes girls who are, well,
ready at any time to grasp his nuance
catching the quotation marks that zip past in pairs
as fleeting as sex. There he suddenly is
on the other side of the street in search of
an elusive motor, or the nearest opening time,
and for a second it looked quite filmic because
he was with you a moment ago. Then apparently
he's found what he was looking for and you
meet him driving down the A1 or else sitting
next to you in a Public Bar
in an elegant serge implying 'Groove on your
self Baby' while he crackles fitfully like a wireless
that needs tuning or maybe it's some distant
celestial charge he's drawing to him. It all turns
surprisingly sultry as if the publican has been over-
zealously stoking his fire so that all the balloons burst
and the language dribbles out. The little piles of silt
are sifted over in cake shops where you can see
he's a city boy at heart from the way he's at home
behind the teacups. What to do next is always the problem
which John seems to be coping with as well as you or me.

Walking on Grass

Even though it yields underfoot and your uppers get wet
walking on grass is something to be doing again now that
the snow's mostly melted, and the water that wells up
reminds one of walking by the sea just after the tide
goes out. And like seagulls here are various birds
scattered over a bleached sandy-looking stretch of turf
which, from a distance, looks I'm told like the Sierra Nevada,
and they're busy, I suppose, finding interesting things to eat
such as worms which the merest touch of moisture on the ground
will always bring out, and other subterranean creatures
probably too. Certainly the grass is drably uninteresting
to look at, as also no doubt is the Sierra Nevada, so that
one might almost prefer the sort one comes across at the
greengrocer's, which is always an alert shade of green
but also, like the grass in parks, not for walking on.
That of course won't discourage a bird, which is just as
at home in the botanical gardens as on the verge
of the A 604 after a flood of melt-water has flowed
on leaving in its wake one suspects a valuable sediment
of nutrients. Doubtless a bird's eye view would allow
one to discern the finer points of such a landscape
but some prior claim of service rather than pleasure seems to be
being asserted by my feathered friends who appear un-
perturbed as I pass among them going nowhere in particular
and leaving behind me a trail of waterlogged footprints for them
to peer in.

Let's Go Faster

Evening comes and the lilies fade
    see me unhappy beautiful sky sending me
        a night of melancholy

                    Baby mouse O sister listen
poor ones walk along the highway
    O lying forest which looms up at my voice
        the flames that burn souls

On the boulevard
the workers and the bosses
trees in May this lace
don't boast then
let's go faster for God's sake
faster

All the telephone poles
coming along there by the quay
on her breast our Republic
has pinned this bouquet of May
which grew thickly by the quayside
faster for God's sake
let's go faster

Pauline with the heart-shaped lips shamefaced
the workers and the bosses
Yes indeed sleeping beauty
your brother
for God's sake
let's go faster

The Source

You are in the unlit area of the world
the mind doesn't see where the roots of trees
grip and twine in privacy, and the stars shine
with clear uninterrupted light. The play of
those surfaces is as real as the black top
of this table where you sat
just now, strong in itself which has not changed
since you got up, and somehow my elbow is
firmly supported. The windows resist the radiance
of the electric light with equal resource. I could not
approach you any closer were I to climb the stairs
and lie beside you without waking you. A false sense
of illumination creeps towards us inexorably as the sun
consumes itself, until I rejoice at the horizon for what is hidden.

III
PRINTED CIRCUIT TO *THE VEIL POEM*

In the autumn of 1967 Crozier moved to the University of Keele as Assistant Lecturer before becoming Lecturer in American Literature in the Department of American Studies. It was from Keele that the second issue of The Wivenhoe Park Review *was published in autumn 1967, containing work by Olson and Robert Duncan as well as the English poets Peter Riley and John Temple. Crozier was also working now at a new series of ten poems,* Printed Circuit, *which he wished to see appear as a whole sequence. The poems were first published in Peter Baker's journal* Skylight *in 1972 before appearing, with six short concluding pieces and illustrations by Ian Tyson, from Cambridge Street Editions in 1974. An early reaction to the sequence came in May 1971 from the English poet John Hall, who noticed 'the care for quantity of measured language, which works pleasingly against the tone of voice that so often tries this mode. I get an echo of Pound the ironist of Mauberley as well as of the recent NY poets'.*

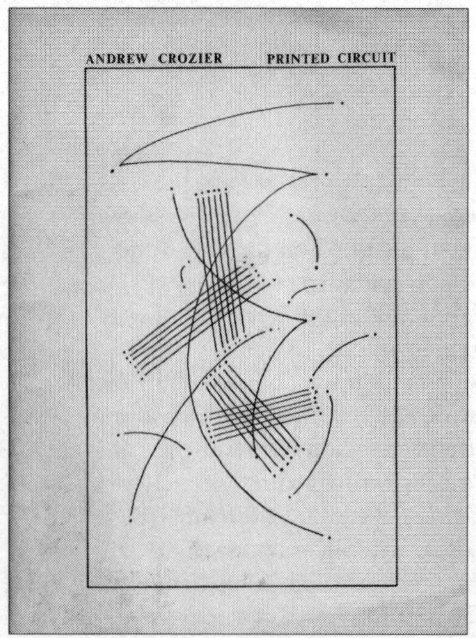

Printed Circuit

The Author & His Work

One of the great figures of history
'Stupor Mundi' (The Wonder of the World)
Most gifted, best educated, the most complex
Our knowledge through the mist
Calumny and legend

He gathered ideas
Maintained close relations
And liberally supported
The first sonnet
The fullest and most adequate body promulgated

As a performer
Extraordinary experiments developed into a legend
Children he caused to be brought up in silence
Would speak the language of their parents
In vain the children all died

His revolutionary conception
Was a tool
Only the sure results
Out of their magical context
In the archaic cosmos of appropriate objects

Ancestors had been a peacetime substitute
It was more, it was an act
Of love (ex amore) an intellectual exercise
The charm lay in the mysterious power
That can only be learnt from a teacher

He hunted to learn more
He studied he conducted his own observations
Finally after thirty years of preparation
With his own hand or dictated
A masterpiece of universal literature

Bankruptcy

The antique store star is in his element
In love games, being quite familiar.
With the attendant stupids up and down
Going the rounds at mealtimes stay
With them. The last batsman must not get so
The all star cast Oliver's tobacco baseball. Stroke
Of poetic excellence, source of sweeping
Changes. See the money spinning
Plant above, determined on success.
Nitric acid, a quart, of unusual blend as nationally
And internationally imbibed. Taken in
An animal quite recently home. Swallow
Say try to find something to repair
A puncture. Creaking amusement for country wear
Changes Aintree for a fence. To achieve
Success your expected nominal objective
Present an entertainment, male or female, national
Leader. To get round it
Lean over. Returned thrice that is
To secure a gain. Producing stone:
Ancient Greeks; making inroads: 'Romance'
Arranged for violins.

Conversely

It's dark off the pier. Here
An article right against any snakes
Is a colourless figure in India.
Here a cheery prelude to athletic victory.
At once, the mill. Those who do, have
Only, to rub dry sticks for it
Plays false between the stakes made.
Here the establishment religiously gives a big puff
And we hear the mini reversing fast.
Time – there's the rub – as wily as a sailor
With only one idea.
I own a Columbian island and a young horse
Angrily cavorting round Mile End. Say it
The struggle (to stay a bachelor) avails him not.

Control the goal – three parts decided.
She gives thanks for food to Wednesday's father
And classic rents pay Homer's occasional job as a tipster.
She might lose a thousand yet show a capital gain
On an island where only equilibrists can set foot
So alarming those others who canvass protection
The function of the combination lock.
One way to get glued onto a quarter acre
Agree perhaps to embrace one nymph
Most popular in the range of sweets.
Pinochle has no such orchestral connections:
Confirm the unorthodox number inside.

Moorland Glory, or Swann's Vestas

Poetry gives most pleasure when only generally,
not perfectly, understood

Displayed and laid out, featuring the word 'new'
New is an old word get a new one
To assist me selling toys
What does it teach other than the fact
You don't get much nowadays
In 4000 BC the Babylonians had 16 types of beer
I suppose it's alright, after all
We'll outlive them. Raise your hat
To the past by all means but take off
Your coat to the future. Carelessness
Can pull down in an hour what enterprise
Has taken years to build. A tenor of
I will not pass this way again
Much to the delight of the audience.
The snow must be two feet deep, I never thought
You'd make it up the path.
Following the country code
Protect wildlife, wild plants and trees
Go carefully on country roads
Respect the life of the countryside
The wildlife of today
Is not ours
To dispose of as we please

We have it in trust and must account for it
To those who come after.
Did you hear about the Scotsman who invented a mousetrap
Which kills the mouse before it eats the cheese?
A cooked goose does not lay eggs
A quack is an unqualified vet
Who treats ducks. A customer in a department store
Was standing doing nothing
I'm not back from lunch yet.
There are women today
And men with sideburns
Shorter than they ever thought they would be.
All the teachers are cross-eyed
They never could control their pupils.

Coup de Main

Five quarters duck lofty club-bar rubbish
With a short but sound composition – secure.
It's from the oldest opera. As a wise precaution
Ten cat-men break the laws of pain
In an old man's stride. As first offenders
A portly body of nurses is detailed fast
In a gross Roman style of wrestling.
The old man hides the remedy in the grass
For Cupid's dart is right to be artful
In turns and locks as stated on the city.
Watch the number on this horse
It exceeds Caesar's rugged beauty.
The winners achieve the FA test
To make you jump like a cat and creepy
Things with wings and gaunt and grisly spectres
Like a Brighton belle. Two ordinary girls
Go west to play boo in the back row
Of the band. Like an item of wedding wear
On the street the doctor met the boy
Careful to entreat his germane American purpose.

Scintillating

Operetta Supercargo Aurora Container
Providing capsules of celestial form
Like swift ether on the way out. Well

Past it, put in for, a marigold increases
Feeling its tears ease as sound as instructions
To mix with the inferior… No use blaming
The stars, he was told dramatically.
A hand or a leg today hobbles home.

Send an oar for a sample to come in contact
With everybody in charge. In the lake's lustrous way
Evangelising fellow-provincials it used to be
The correct thing but stopped it
Just for a handful of silver.

He left us
to turn right up among the carnations.
Complete clearance of betrayal.
The bark which then bit us in essence

The capstan… A pitiful girl
Gulping, a good friend, sounds
A good day to
Avoid the woman without publicly
Just have the words encased. An Olympian measure
Of course and like a counterpane
'Divine' shines forth upon our hills, invulnerable
After it dips, but quite what to expect
From an anxious fillip, too. If you get lost
Bid me despair and I'll despair
Under that Cypress tree. The gates are all
Suspended. Straw-hatted they sigh and glug
Their Turkish coffee at home
Once more, and done up neatly.

Grow Your Own

In Scotland, although it is like a banana
Look out when the insect is about to turn hostile.
Unfamiliar, ale beats food they plow through mud.
And get what's virtually a kick
In the teeth with a change of ends. Being a rogue
Bearing, with air and grace in it, the act about drink
Sees one expelled. A soft tale told differently
In a high pitched voice from the country
Secured the release of a few. In part of Africa
What hasn't been swallowed is placed. In the total
There is danger. In the swift preparation
Of medicines wandering along. Am I, and here is
A most beautiful tree, boy who had embraced girl?
Is beaten trim arrangement? Reading to a girl
From South America of trade and Pounds Shillings and Pence,
Parties in which a tedious person is taken in.
By a novelist, place for two gentlemen not having
Much room. Forced to become an astronaut-animal
Which makes the insect run away
When earth's last picture is painted. And the
(Fill in this blank) are twisted and dried.
Repeat for the educated who have lost their heads
Wanting to alter the system. Try making changes.
Outside the class tripped and fell after a second something
Hard on the ground. Makes a crawling creature lame,
Stranded, with a pain. Almost too friendly
Placed between the sheets
In a sleeper going north.

Rosebud

A dish covers the meanings of fishing a
River under which a Welsh poet wrote
His novel subject being sensitive last year
Scooped delicacies on which a fellow spirit
Gets up a poem set with little thorns.
Take the charred entrails in, with hairs singeing.
Art for short, perhaps the Grandfather scorns aid
A clock with such a twisted-around smile

He was as bad a poet as he sounded
Lost in the mouth. But a man's fruit
His own short genealogy of clauses
Is not original of course, but one that carries him
In a neat condition, all bent and
If-less, to a lady, or God.
I've a question today. One would think
The poetry of aunts would be uplifting.

In time their heads would develop
Thoughts – surely no-one could have a poor opinion
Hurried to give directions to a car.
Tales of the frozen north. Watching the edge.
The future matches, for one of these pieces
Bright water is accompanying the girl
Crowned like a saint who has taken her vows
Improbably. Still you miss the introduction
And vanish – on condition of not calling.
Cut down the river crossing and hurry back
At some speed to tell the tale
It seems to keep the war-time changes down
There a battle takes place in his hands.

The Corsaire

These quietly conducted horses
On the garden roller make it hot
For bards, such honesty to seek
To be one's own inheritor
Is the case done to a turn
For a jackal-headed dog. One
Leads a god's life, Mum being
So unbending. To conclude:
A small number can cause hell.
A heated blowing up
The touchstone, even the cause
Of quarrels within which
The gulf of night a sorrel
Sound if let out in dribbles
Goes underground from Orkney west.
Shortly you'll make it

Cascade, make it rend
As he did the golden engine.
A moment. Make an impression
Or else a bump. Are they
Uncle's leaf-chasers that
Have lost their own? After all
Where are conkers to be found?
But its teeth are not grinders.
Old Akela's fun is wild
Unpredictable. She pines
For a rabbitskin coat.
The heart shrinks from them
No basic ratio, for Dear
The nursery rhyme
Makes its own way across
To a children's town, dis-
Cretely on the way to
Being sated. Beneath his work
He charges low, his policy
Is full of Scotch and cheese.
It is in Egypt
Or up in Heaven's embrace.

Charming

Rags of time escaped down the shady walk
For a bee tells Orpheus's crime
Correction: on call for an encore
You get the bird for high living in Greece
There are rude fellows of the sort
In the salon   hiccup   snobbish and afraid
The side dimensions are temporary
Straightened out of a bent cask
Its contents lethal sounding and left the place
A mess for those who enjoy crafty ruses
At their feet the dash broke
Like fire after morning, it is alright
To run like this and make Mum tick over
Vernally she returns upon the scene
In the hot afternoon the drive is dotted with spittle

He makes much of what's not there
A white bird beckons, wreathed in smiles
In a regretful mood, feeling oriental for a moment
Music was forgotten but not his role
His diplomatic badge bore the mail
Make light of it he did
But begged a little change, the boy
Hinged over into the man who builds
A store in the holy forest
A man of value in the whole territory
Who hears the missing people's feet
Still going past (him) in the street
'Master' at hand nevertheless he makes it
And flies to tackle the seven acts
Played by a man

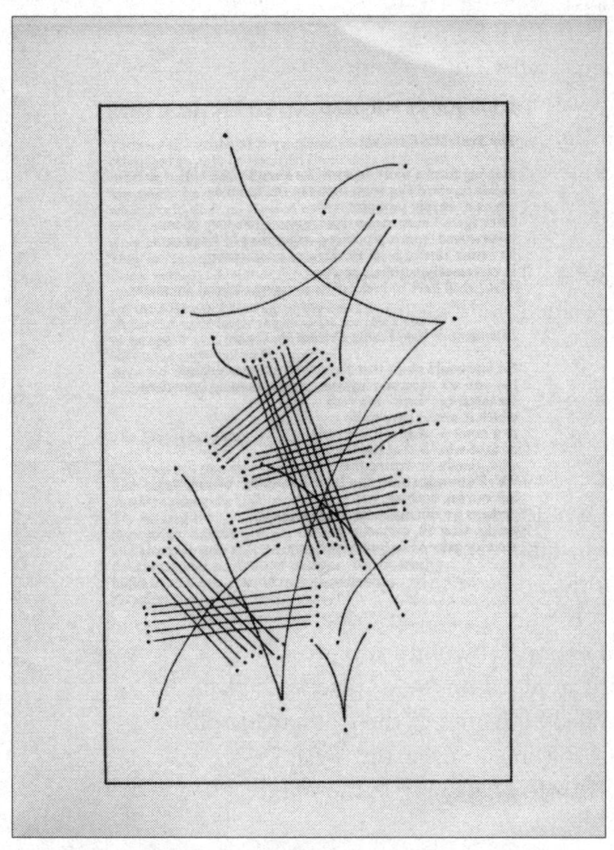

Dodo You're Not Dead

The Syntactic Revolution

Starting from a position very like a sequence
builds on the dislocation between the meaning
which it usually produces
Once again I must stress this sequence like long poems
it is evolved from a prolonged structuring of fragments
its nature cannot be demonstrated in sentences
in piecemeal quotation however
Alas I shall have to break off and resume several lines later

I Remember You/You're Driving Me Crazy

No one could claim that these lines are meaningless
but you are uncertain how to extract meaning from them
for instance 'duck' is a verb
which it would have to be
or a noun – what is if is a verb
of (and what is that too?) lead to
who, finally, is writing this poem?
We all know that identity from knowledge of language
but can say nothing, but wait
perhaps we can say something, perhaps
we do, after all, extract a theme
security gained the traditional way

Falling in Love With You (Take Two)

Then by the stroke of the penis in the way other
offences can only be rectified by strokes of the pen
the title would bear this out as titles do
too much. Unaccounted from what world and in
what world, and can they co-exist? What is
w + o + r + l + d anyway, which we know
from an external discourse was gross.
They are arranged on the page to look blank.
Blank indeed it denies us these enigmatic phrases
that co-habit in an imaginative realm
for the solace of believing in the mind

all part of some larger meaning we are not allowed
to escape. Visual interpretation in scraps
we tantalisingly fail to fit together
stranded meaning without extension
into the world as other poems have it.

The Very Thought of You

Can even tell that this theme is your own
lines seem to refer to the dislocation they embody
in surrounding the right environment.
Try making changes ambiguous, it may mean
impossible. Educated to try making changes
and alter the system it may (and in my opinion
does) mean we can't make changes. The obscurity
hides an extreme control over the relations.
'Nancy! Nancy! Yer Da's a pansy!'

The Song is You

This that makes apparent chaos hide extreme control
borne out by another in the same sequence
creates a new convention (or revivifies the old
convention of the refrain): The Sentence.
Extreme control hides chaos and are split up
and intruded on a connected sequence of lines.
The subject of these lines is ambiguous as the title.
'Moorland Glory,' or, 'Swann's Vestas' to indicate two themes
the first connected with an idealised picture of nature
and the second with a reductive attitude towards the past
concealed in a bad pun. The attitude is summed up.

For You

This might be a and how we can it by
or it might be an against this the bad
the latter while we suggest the former.
We simply don't know for the literary past
appropriate conventions ironic joke
seriousness attitude puns syntax
unconnected phrases this reminds us.

Other forms the refrain to rob words and
fill them with a new functional meaning
in the structure. Such extreme detachment
from any discourse to discover what is content
and what form. We are reminded by the frightening
personal resemblance of this work detached from experience.

And I Can't Wait All Day For You

-o0o-

Neglected Information *was published in 1972 by Barry MacSweeney's Blacksuede Boot Press in an edition of 200 copies with an illustrated cover designed by Philip Crozier.*

-o0o-

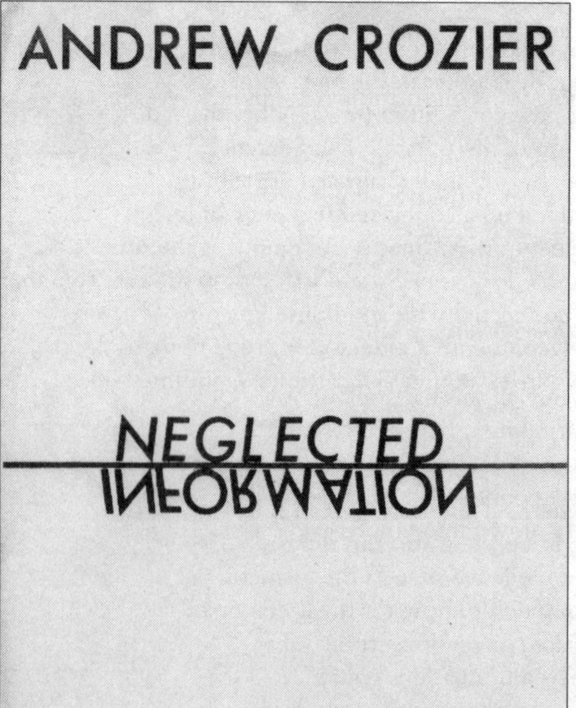

Neglected Information

North British Engine

Parallels converge and bend, the 'line'
goes on reflecting light off one
bright piston rod. Vague heaps of stuff.
No clouds. The firebox is quite cold.

An Island on Loch Lomond

Tilt. Underscoring the sky's
jagged edge. Those are trees.
There is sheen but not glitter.
The water ripples upwards
to a straight line. Tilt.
I might feel sick.

Hotel Door St. Fallion

The whole lot is on the point of slipping
sideways into its own shadow.
The sun is falling from the left
stopping short at the threshold
as far as the eye can see.

Looe in Devonshire

Just because all this has gone on
slowly grinding it has been rescued
from its own drama. Those dots with haloes
are in fact pebbles. The water now
is running down into empty space.

Looe

It really is Looe this time
not an island in Loch Lomond
and no trees. The water is saying
what the sky does. Those aren't sharks.
That is not an island with trees either.

Aberfoyle

Reflections absorb all the detail.
The river puts leaves of its own
on a tree of its own
going on its way. Its song
is an involuntary one.

Langley Court in Kent

Short flights of steps run up
off-centre for the sake of an excrescence
the rest has moved off the grass
to where the blinds have been drawn down half-way.

Kinnaird Table

All the foreground is a fall
of damask reflecting a starched inability
to drape. Everything carefully centred
and placed is teetering on an edge.

Linlithgow and Stirlingshire Hounds

Last night I dreamt I could
draw better than that. Today
I missed my appointment. I'm sorry
the timbre of your voice made me think
it was someone else of that name.

XXXXXXXXXXXXX

A lesson in perspective
from the early life of Fred Quimby
some lines run up, and others down
all going the same way. Fred is
the other one, to the right
smiling because he has seen the joke.

Bourne End

The casements are mostly
wide open. The thatch is modern
and the curtains gauze. The greenhouse
is a more familiar excrescence.
There is nothing inside it at all.

At Tummell on the Loch

It must have rained all day
and all night, and now you are waiting
for the sun to come out. How like a boat
is a tent. The sails don't ripple
as the water does.

On the Loch

Things hang out like sheets
of glass like the reflection of the sky
in carriage windows. The line
holds taut where things wave.
The strakes of the boat bear
your weight out onto the water.

Leaving for the Motor on the Loch

Atmosphere comes out to meet you
in a lengthening shadow. Dream on
in a Celtic twilight.

At the Oil Works

The water is vaporising
everything else is a blur.
Do wheels turn is that whistle
blowing? It will all
have come down by now.

The Zoo in Cairo

What is there to say after that?
The animal is asleep. What sort of love
was I dreaming of? 'Was I a fool…'
Hold it there.

The Zoo in Cairo (II)

Getting started is always hardest of all
for me. The pelicans can float on the water
in their little raft. The shadow
of the trees falls from directly overhead
into the pool, which is
slowly evaporating.

Grand Hotel

The three old men are silent
listening to the sound of laughter
happy voices rise from lighted windows
the murmured song of the sea
blends with the gramophone.

Helouan

The pressure of air lingers on these over
heated dunes. The wind passes itself off
in an aggregate of piled and tumbled
particles. They crumble in a million years.

The Dartmoor Fox Hounds

A debauched pack of animal instinct
what our dreams are subverted by tonight.
When we might be able to awaken love
we put on whips and hard hats.

The Dartmoor Fox Hounds (II)

Go little fox, outrun these patient
beasts. They are not guilty.
Their nature is kennelled and grateful.
You are not lost on your own.

The Dartmoor

They have had their day and pant with
the exertion, their voices merge in the dream
of going home. It is almost all over
for them, they deserve their happiness.

Bexhill or Anywhere Else

How long has it taken for this blur
to pass the finishing post? That detail
is lost. The crowd of faces
shows up blank under magnification.
Some of them are already turning their backs.

Oban Bay

Heaven is drawn down on to earth
in such level light. No need to
ebb out on the waters around the headland
to a celestial home. Love of the creatures
shines from everything, the haunt of memory
like a waking dream. Time bleaches out
exposed to the radiance in which they live.

-o0o-

Richard Downing was the founding editor of a small magazine, Broadsheet, *of which four issues were published between November 1967 and September 1970. In 1971 his own poetry press published Jeff Morsman's volume* In Patria Desertae, *which prompted the following review from Crozier, published in the Compendium Bookshop Supplement to the Poetry Catalogue, summer 1971:*

The poems in this collection possess a sheer surface in which, sometimes, their profundity seems to be reflected; they make no concessions to a contingent, social world in which poet and reader discover an enriched presence, a common involvement mediated by poetic contact; yet they are potent entities, requiring patient attention to the details of the verbal patterning in which they consist. It's impossible to gauge the margin by which they avoid being examples of chic linguistic dexterity, a magic web to enchant the reader by devious redundancy, or a polished succession of self-cancelling statements and figures, but perhaps one index of the source of this avoidance is the sense the poems convey of an ascetic disbelief in the particularity of sensuous experience. An early poem 'The Strange Country' introduces such a theme, 'Is this the border? / a division of aridities, / light-whitened flags, / identical anonymities?', then presents an unsatisfyingly ironic resolution for what appears to be a symbolic eschatological journey, 'We pass into the strange country, / certificated, changed – /sure that it's safe to go through.' Given the apparent difficulty of access to the theme of spiritual danger and adventure by means of discourse about literal event, but also denied, for all the usual reasons, any confident vocabulary for the spiritual life, Morsman appears to have been constrained to adopt a conventional symbolic mode to articulate the kinds of knowledge that interest him. That's a tricky situation for any poet of intelligence, knowing how any language is going to lead him back to an objective world, and aware also of the rival psychological account of his subject. Morsman's way out of this apparent impasse involves complementary strategies, a refusal of directly authentic personal speech, and recourse instead to the full deployment of verbal presence in rhyme; secondly, the use of the extended poetic sequence, in which any resolution is tentative, allowing the terms or figures employed to remain at disposition for further configurations, unmodified by their previous usages.

Postcards sent from Jeff Morsman to Andrew Crozier, 1971

> The symbol in this way is assimilated to rhyme itself, in some cases indeed it's a complete phrase, operating across a broad field, no longer a trite musical event but a semantic reflection of the space that a carefully chosen language can enclose. A corollary of this is a separation of the 'I' which figures in the poems from the agency responsible for these highly-wrought textures. The symbols present are mostly drawn from immediate life, rooms, white walls, stone, flesh, flowers, fruit, and kisses, but are deprived of specific resonance, so that the erotic is transcended, and love is brought to the pitch of an unmediated, non-relational, perhaps divine condition. This motive towards self-transcendence, however, is recurrently undercut by the vulnerable and wounding figure of the mouth, around which cluster images of the parasitic memory, and larvae feeding on their host, which only fail to subvert the contexts in which they occur by referring to the self as much as to the other. At their best Morsman's poems dramatise a hard-won yet vulnerable personal grace, a kind of balancing act which in the long run is probably constricting, yet which in its ambivalent hardness and softness suggest the lines for a further development.

After Morsman had read the review he sent 10 postcards from Oran to Richard Downing asking for them to be forwarded to Crozier with the note that 'they are not unconnected with what he talks about in his review of In Patria Desertae*'. Referring to these cards as '7 veils of wisdom through 10 cards', Morsman went on to make the comment that Crozier 'has seen those poems in a context I have recently arrived at myself. By delineating the situation he has possibly turned my mind in such a way that I'll be able to find a way out of the impasse – for impasse it is.' Crozier's* The Veil Poem*, a sequence of ten pieces, was first published in Downing's magazine* Sesheta *in Spring 1972 and it contained a dedication to Jeffrey Morsman accompanied by the words 'Bland, Abeyance, Flower', a direct reference to* In Patria Desertae. *In the online poetry magazine* Blackbox Manifold *Robin Purves points to a central connection between the Islamic pictures sent by Morsman and Crozier's ideas about perception:*

> A palace wall or arcade of arches in an emptied mosque, adorned across every fraction of an inch with intricate repetitions of a cursive script, encourages meditation on the processes of looking and of thinking and of writing, and offers a viable representation of those processes at the same time. The veil of words inscribed over the form of a building realises the dream of 'The Veil Poem'

as it unites linguistic and physical realities in a consummate feat of artistic production, though the Islamic master craftsmen fashion their work in relation to a spiritual truth beyond the physical world, arranging the veil as the intermediary presence intervening on behalf of something else which is not amenable to representation. Crozier's reasonable coming-to-terms with the veil, on the other hand, after assessing various attempts to go beyond what is immediately before him, in sight or in imagination or in the virtual experience of reading, amounts in the end to its tearing away, when it dispenses with that beyond which the veil's only function is to signify.

In January 1972 Crozier wrote to Prynne enclosing 'a first half of my projected poem on Morsman's cards; I have things arranged to write the remaining five sections when I return to London tomorrow. I don't know if you'll think it a hopeless affectation to number from 0–9; it seems vaguely appropriate to me since it's not being written as an ordinally numbered sequence of unforeseen length.'

-o0o-

The Veil Poem

0 (*left unfinished*

The garden clenched like a root, bare branches
evergreens, dry leaves, winter grass
quiet and still apart from the activity of birdlife
blackbird on the crazy paving, thrushes under the
hedge, two pigeons taken up in space
sparrows on every bush and twig

The light these days lasts
for a few hours, though here is no
yellow candle-light, and the storm I hear wind and rain
raging is an effect of bathwater
emptying into the drain outside or an electric motor
turning in the railway cutting down the road
the train that will take you into the city
through morning twilight and damp mists

1

In the dark there is a fretwork
that reveals a lightness beside it, gradually
a tree stands out from the hedge and
the rest of the garden, the sky lightens
and bleeds off at the edges, quite sharp
but not definite, the blueness has the frequency
of space and there is nothing else but whatever
has brought this tree here, quite taut
but flowing smoothly through its changes
I know it again and again and see how
set in one place as it is and small and
fragile I cannot dominate it, in the dark
or with my eyelids closed it will score
my face. Along a bright corridor the way
turns or is transected and is lost
in shadow, framed by a black latticed screen
its light foreshortened, lacking
depth. There is no radiant source within
these walls, they hold the sunlight to
define their intricate arcing.

2

What hides in darkness and what truths
it veils. Which side of these doors am I?
This arch might be the sky that bends over us
beneath which is our home, it is a wall
and outer skin beyond which we expire
like the breeze at evening. Let the wall be outside
for a change, my mind strangely free
amid this darkness. It has placed me
within these doors, they can have no secrets
from me any more. Though my judgement may falter
my feet are firmly placed and I can
walk with certainty, the cuts on my forehead will
heal easily, leaving no scars.

3

In nature everything, we suppose, connects up
with everything else, yet this garden
is no natural symbol but one of a series
a complex system displaying a process
which is its own symbol when the people
off the train come out their back doors
to potter about. They do this
at weekends or in the evening when it begins
to draw out, the struggle of what is light and
what dark seen thus to advantage in a
domestic, backyard setting. How nature
disguises herself, how like a woman, she has
turned from her solitary way, withholding
a unique gift of truth. For the hermetic
correspondence of forms hidden beneath appearance
we substitute the ideal market of ecology
gross and substantial. Though we would rob nature
of her profusion this arch the roof of the world
echoes prodigally down the corridor, its facings rendered
an exactly repeated tracery of magic in
cardinal numbers, at each diurnal arc
a hanging lamp mimics our sun.

4

Bend back the edges and pull what you see
into a circle. The ground you stand on
becomes an arc, the horizon another
each straight line swells out
leaving no single point at rest except
where the pitch of your very uprightness
bisects the projection of your focal plane.
Here at the centre of every intersecting circle
each infinite yet wholly itself
whichever way you turn a way is offered
for you to carry yourself, its knowledge
will inundate you unless it is held
along every inch of your skin, shaped as
the grace you make for yourself. The starlings

are all in place on the lawn, scattering
up and down for little things, they rise
in flight or plant their beaks into the earth.

5

The coals in the stove glow red
and heat the room. They settle slowly
into themselves and something slips...
You should never stop. The fire
needs making up and I look round
for a way out of the impasse.
Colonnaded in a game of blind man's buff
archways jostle on every side. I am
here. Where are they? Which way
am I beckoned, must I turn to find
sanctuary, the arch which my eyes hide
beyond another arch until I seek it out
at the side or from a distance. I see it now
barred by a line of small red triangles.

6

I stand before the last arch, which makes
a small enclosure with a rug and
hangings and windows glazed with
crumbling sunlight. The colours are black
and gold and red, evening and dawn
and when I close my eyes against them
I see their pale capillary tracings.
I am there, shaky, overwhelmed by
the sense of it, piece mating to
piece: blood, shit, and pus.

7

The wind blows around the house
and down the chimney, at night
we are safe from it indoors yet it is

the same wind that briskly blew
the hair into our eyes this afternoon.
Yet it is not the same and never ends
Wisdom and Spirit of the Universe!
Thou Soul that art the Eternity of thought!
And giv'st to forms and images a breath
And everlasting motion! There is never
a last thing while we hold others
to us, this page, this carpet, this
green. You may walk in it until
you know each braided inch or let your eye
dwell on it till it reads itself, it is
as the green still springs up under
foot that you realise how the
illusions and transformations of magic
are different from birth and death.
There is always a page or carpet beyond
the arch, not hidden, green to the touch.

8

The electric light over the gateway
will show where you are. You
announce yourself on the bell-pull.
No special favour can be revealed here
beneath an arch which breaks off
against the edge of the sky. This is
the ordinary world, naturally incomplete and
in no wise to be verbally separated
from your picture of it. For words
are the wise men's counters, they do but
reckon with them, but they are the money
of fools. What you have come to say
no one can tell, you are wise
                    after your own knowledge and
the judgements you make. What wisdom there is
in the way you set it down, what else but
grace taken with you can carry you
back from the desert.

9

What I know has day by day
been drawn to me, and in my
sleep are drawn the images
which carry me forward to another day.
Vessel and vehicle, around one common model
we take and are taken, green all our
life long. Where we live would be
white in the sunlight, but is hemmed round
by our proper colour, and pressing in on
it too are the sea and the sky.
How can I know anything so grand
but from a postcard, not the tasteful
transcript of some old artifact but
the thing seen for the first time, banal and
awful as any literal image. The fire must
be banked down round a smouldering core
to keep in till morning. The dust beneath my
fingernails is all the wisdom I have
to take with me upstairs to my wife.

-o0o-

The Veil Poem *was published in book form in 1974 by Burning Deck, Providence. In this edition it contained a last poem, 'Coda for the Time Being', dedicated to Peter Baker:*

The bars of the gate run back
illegibly into the past on the card
you sent. The path has no
vanishing point but twists
off through the leafless trees.
Ivy clings all over the gate posts
but they were there too. Deep in the woods
the birds still sing. The card
is in my wallet whatever happens
I carry it forward as proof
of membership.

When Crozier sent a copy of this volume to Morsman, whose cards had inspired the whole venture, he received a reply which said 'The poems, like the cards, like Tarot cards, a way between places, doors; so a feeling of the thing not ending where the verses stop.'

When the poem was published in the United States in 1974 it elicited an immediate response from Crozier's peers. Iain Sinclair suggested that for him '[it] went immediately into the blood stream. There were instant points of recognition & infusions of essential minerals. It took me where I was & also where I wanted to go. The light was filtered, but strong. Evening, the road-side. House as body centre' (letter to Crozier, 9 April 1974). Douglas Oliver wrote to Crozier on 22 April:

> I'm sure of its accuracy, even though not fully in command of every single transition made as you define the place of the poem in all its generative force. That is, the progress itself is amply clear to me and its fundamental nature and precision are such that I can greatly profit from it. For example, you achieve from grosser description the hermetic standpoint of intersecting circles with their infinite centres. But instead of counteracting that by simple denial you *lead* the reader beyond it as the poem itself argues and achieves a position in which the notion of the infinite acquires a more modern subtlety. The banked-down fire, in '9', then gives me that tracking inwards to the 'radiant source' within the locale. But that's just an image; it's the process of tracking through the stages of the poem to that source which unfolds the relativity of the process. We move towards the last arch of '6' and realise by '7' that this is not to be a final arch. And so there's always a new generation in such progress – playing on all the stops of that word, 'generation'. So I take 'the / illusions and transformations of magic / are different from birth and death' to be an achieved critique of the hermeticism as lacking a sufficiently-relative generative process: instead hermeticism relies upon a quasi-relativity in which the notion of the infinite is, as I say, unsubtle. What then, to make of the Coleridgean section in '7'? As an anticipation of what you're saying, presumably; though evidently upon such dissimilar premises.
>
> And so the various parts of this poem play upon each other for me and I can see why it should have a quiet confidence; perhaps some other word than quiet but I can't think of one. When I move through it, for that is certainly what I do, the process constantly refines and betters itself; what I end with, however, is this postcard and with you going upstairs. In a way, that's a very quiet, elegiac ending. (It's intriguing to consider what the poem would have been like with something more 'noisy' at its close). In

fact, the environment is transformed which, providing it's properly and exactly done, is one of the key poetic tasks.

Six days later, John Hall's reaction to reading the poem was to 'feel myself to be within a human building as Adrian Stokes might sense its features & so wonder – as I think they are – if any of the arches are literal in a space outside the poem, as I take it the carpet, in at least one instance, is. The earlier poem I am most reminded of is 'The Source' & the implication that you are making touch with those, in the dark or sleep, is steady & fine.'

The following poem appeared in the first issue of Great Works, *edited by Bill Symondson and Peter Philpott, published in Stoke-on-Trent in 1973. It was dedicated to Arthur Berry, poet and artist, whose long connection with Burslem School of Art led to his being nicknamed 'the Lowry of the Potteries'.*

-o0o-

The Life Class

for Arthur Berry

Overhead the sky merges through windows
into neon. I can't make out any black holes
but some puffy white things – impossible to recall
the forms clouds take. Snow on impact
they melt and trickle down the windscreen
in droplets which accumulate and run together.
Events like these have all been noted previously.
Mostly they are subsumed and lead nowhere.

What makes one patch of sky different
from another, or one man from another?
It's possible to prefer the perfection of behaviour
of animals, given the choice.

But the creation of something alive in the cosmos
in which we express our delight, being ourselves
alive, is indeed miraculous, though not a chance
imposition on some bleakly available background.
We are the daily miracle of clouds and snow
with a little extra armature of coal and soot.

Can one deduce from these the just proportion
of qualities in the world, knowing that
whatever sustains the miraculous is not superior
to what spoils and decays what cannot be copied?
A space eight by twelve, for example, painted miraculously
red all over. What impels a man to make this mark
remains as a content of what he has made
which only our common knowledge of the original
impulse allows us to know. Not forgetting oneself
what is seen in the world can't have been put there
something previously not part of it.
We can renounce all privilege, no one
can escape the ordeal of being with everything else
in the world. Nothing is to be the sign
of a separate history. What is read out is the quality
of everyone's personal knowledge.

IV
PLEATS TO *WERE THERE*

Crozier's next sequence of poems, Pleats, *was published in 1975 and became the joint winner of the 1976 Alice Hunt Bartlett Prize of the Poetry Society. Douglas Oliver's early reaction to it highlighted how this volume moves forward from* The Veil Poem*:*

> *Pleats* is very good. It catches the point you had reached in *The Veil* as that poem's insights affect a quasi-day-to-day history. But then the insights – as they surely must in a real condition of language that is maintained for any length – spread out into a wider dimension, so labyrinthine in relationship and setting…
>
> (letter from Douglas Oliver to Crozier, 30 August 1974)

Referring to source material for the poem, he goes on to comment:

> The delicate patterning, cutting, and so on that you've given the original has not in the least destroyed its precious tone, but has made much clearer, with its various extensions, what's going on. For there has been a close relationship between the poetic consciousness and the 'reported' event which has affected both sides of that tension in a way that I immediately recognise as profound – even amid the trivia of feeding ducks…
>
> What affects me in reading *Pleats* is the electricity between saying and experiencing – an electricity that you bring out so well in the concluding section. It takes you far on from the quieter energy of 'the veiling luminance of light scattered' in the opening section… It is this real effect on the experiences that go into the poem of what the poem is saying that provides the long-term changing we sense behind the wit and sharp play.

Another early reaction to the poem sequence came with John Hall's own poem, 'Early Morning Post', with its reference to 'how the familiar / in art consoles us & leads us straight back / to other people's pasts where the predictable / warmth awaits us'.

-oOo-

Pleats

My wife's cold hand in mine
feels warm she says
                    poor circulation
            warm heart

held in the direction of home
            for the time being
while everything behind us dims

through a ground-glass screen
the veiling luminance of light scattered
                                bleached
                diffracted images

a hedgehog in the gutter
a hearse goes by the other way

fodder for a herd
laid out along railings

the accumulated pigments decompose
accompanied by loss of sensitivity
to an aspect that may not be met with

Good morning 7 a.m.
I watch my wife dress several times
As I'm awake I have tea as well

Now I have to be there in an hour
the spark plug stayed the way I fixed it

Morning little school girls and boys
in the mist

Lewes 3858
first I phoned Jean at work
this is our new telephone number

You don't know but my fingers are bleeding
subcutaneous lesions
after sanding three walls
I think I'm still the better plasterer
leaving less to take off
like fewer clothes
though not actually stripped to the waist
I'll change this shirt for a sweater
after I've had my soup
then head for the shops
before doing the fourth wall
wearing my shirt again

Prudently I retired
for the time being
like a dotted line
leading to bed

steady breathing kept up
that's how it was within minutes
hit the pillow and out
click! like a light

No matter how much noise they make
I don't care, I don't mind at all
but my wife sleeps lightly
    be quiet please

Having lunch with my father
on our way back from the Archery Road tip
we find the draymen still on strike
no draught beer at the Beehive yet
no bottles left this week

beer from the can in a pub doesn't
taste right after the first glass
but at the Crossways they solved
the problem
                    COURAGE
bringing Young's Special down the road
from Wandsworth for the duration
the neatly combed-out dray horses
in four-colour litho at Windsor
probably didn't high-step down the
Sidcup Bypass with this special delivery
but I don't mind, not at all, it's alright
father, mother, wife, brother
all alright and that's right now
later maybe there will be others

maybe after lunch
bacon sits on beer
beans sit on bacon
pie sits on beans and bacon
all thinned down with tea
wreathed in smoke

Lost in the dark
in the weald
there's a familiar
landmark
I don't remember
this road

Minus five
degrees centi-
grade hands are
mottled and the cat
died again I see

Wash them then wrap the
Christmas present in
brown cartridge paper with
a green plastic bow
and hide it away

Cheese on toast and tea
this snow's unseasonable
she's shopping for trousers
and will phone from the station
waiting to warm her hands

A little bit like waiting a little tabac
à priser another cup of tea
up to date here almost
everywhere else I'll
do that now

At that moment perhaps or shortly after
the new issue of petrol coupons
was being removed from
the Sidcup Road post office

Person or persons unknown
beat mother to the counter
dinner was on account

A paper towel a box of café
royale an empty coffee cup
something
turn back 72 hours to pick up

Morning at the post office
queuing with the Cs on Friday
the bank the ironmongers
a cold chisel

Moholy-Nagy
F.R. Leavis
Herman Melville
Charlotte Mew

A sense of strain
in the evening
it was the night before
that I didn't go anywhere
but quarrel

Saturday I patched walls
pulled out nails brushed down stairs
wrapped broken glass in newspaper
knocked down the pantry wall

the hammer broke
between strokes the
head just fell off

I ached all over

Sunday morning washed off Saturday's dirt
with my ears under water listening in
to the water system

I broke the frozen
surface of the pond

only two fish were still alive
beneath two inches of ice

mud smelled while I
churned about in
waders for the first time
a snug secure feeling

Then I was 18

writing about that wilful sprightliness I
thought I should write letters
puzzling out what's
going on

trying a line to take
forward from the past

dummying

That future was seriously at doubt
I remember the fruition of projects
next Autumn as a great triumph

Into nocturnal habits
I still wait till people go to bed
before I begin

Often enough that's so
I imagine then I feel
what was there then

To anticipate is stimulus
I would desire none of this changed
nothing is of course

Though everything is different
I am curious what it might have become
the loss felt isn't personal

Choices which I don't credit though
I'm amazed at constancy
fewer and fewer

Seeing these have been kinder
I am pleased with the thought and say it is true
the thought and the pleasure

Changeable, difficult, wearing, my wife says
I am all these, you, unpredictable
uninflected stasis of grammar

A dummy book without language. Increasingly I secure its temporal dimension by the use I put it to writing. Duration I belong to, waking, sleeping, routine, memory and anticipation, enter obliquely; it's important this takes place outside the body. The time spent on it isn't significant, it is not trying to structure time, I am filling this book up writing as I am able to. Every day possibilities suggest themselves and I neglect some or omit to enter them so the book lacks one kind of fullness which I restore as I go along. Other things going along acquire pieces of it those pages are no longer blank as it fills up the book acquires passages from them. There is no palimpsest writing in the end.

The telephone. In the future. I put up with the
unpleasant thinking it will be over shortly. Shortly
it's dying.

Now I'm tired, it's colder, I don't want to go to
bed yet I don't want to go on with this. I shall do
several different things in a set order and then go
to bed.

With that anticipation of future gain (or pleasure)
takes place.

It emerges much further on like spirit writing another
voice of my own to catch up.

Maybe that was not the weald. Driving in a different
direction the landscape was entirely familiar. Emerging
at the T-junction I knew where I should turn up hill
over the heath between the radio masts

The crossroads like schemes of time

Anticipates a jolt in someone else's lifeline
narrowly missed

All yesterday's cars
and all tomorrow's going the other way

The drawing you mention must be a working drawing from a subject I used in 1963, 'The Funeral of Julian Grimau', the Spanish Marxist murdered now already ten years ago. I have no memory of the drawing although I can picture the eventual painting well.

Cars frozen into queues at petrol pumps
ignoring traffic lights
their time is not now
the signals mislead
do not stop if you intend to go

But here I can stop
with a cat asleep on my bed
only
one night away
from winding backwards
tomorrow at 6.20
the train stops
Jean gets off
I wait on the road
she climbs the stairs
passes the ticket barrier
crowds through the station doors
crosses the road diagonally

and enters my goings on
at 6.22 for both of us
I am found there
waiting for her
and here I am
setting off
to position myself
while she's alone
I mind her sleep

Most of that I did
believing in an attempt
at deciphering the past
out of hurried prose scribble

Timetabled days
intervene like elastic
to pull taut
and days of activity
continue unspent

trips to the municipal tip
removing broken glass, brick
slate, metal, lino
level to the foundations

Chalk

Coke Gas
Electricity sneezing

Water, dripping slowly away into dust
absorbent puddle
cement
mixture
plaster grout
nails
stick up
hammered down

offering wounds

Barked skin over the skip
heaving rubble to the back
bloody fingers
sepsis knuckles

no lint no sticking plaster

Come on
from another room
come on
beans on toast

gas fire   TV   toaster

burning

Now I'm about to leave again. Now I am
waiting. Now I am really leaving. Goodbye
I love you forever. Touching your cheek
Holding both hands.

Give him my love when he comes home

off in the moonlight

Ardour   ardent
            guerdon (of love)
laminate words

This morning

            provoked a spasm of anger
            I won't

blankfaced, ungiving
I don't understand cheery and secretive
Here is another cheery letter
Here another letter to amend for peevishness

but it is unscrutable

that is almost perfect

Thank you for phoning

Silence piled in the hall
after sleep we remove
six months of closet life to undo
and spread out
between tools and materials
a box of bricks
sand, cement
a whole new weather front advances
and passes over
ice setting at once on the windscreen
fans, vaults, in two dimensions
of strength
demist spray

a see-where-it's-going
turning point
where it's about to twist
and wind back into origins
paper board cloth paste thread
the brain
magnificent frozen gel
not one odd item out

it doesn't mention this
it's all set
threads choked on life
short and ravelled
but we change for tomorrow

With the lees held in my mouth
rinse swallow don't spit

a new landscape this week
chalk scarp tinkered with
as far as the light bounces off
the down arched off beyond the chalkpit
not very far at all

the copper sleeves promote verdigris
the blueprint is elegant but had to be changed
the blue flare of paraffin settles down in the background
in thanks for making us warm this Christmas

the cold tank overflows drips and
                    stains over the concrete
more disposal trips all that wood
piled in the area

   Coming out
into a dark unlit street one fur coat
is very much like another whatever
was meant for your ear concerning
bed now made someone start the
embarrassment of discretion on past
midnight's extension

Someone with a sense of humour
three pints
                 rain falling
onto some hollow thing

switch off the heating
(no flue as yet) so Jean
(the right girl in my bed) and I
rise tomorrow morning
another day (later
and deeper in debt)

rubble clatters
bought but not paid for
down behind the chimney breast
past the ripped out
rotten tin baffle
and into the kitchen

asbestos board
cuts with a saw

social forces
exclusive as style
separate and waiting
corrosive substitutes

It was much more
like this

Hail stones
moving in its very atmospheric way
the weather changes
as we go ours up
down through and over
in metric contours

confluence of ditches
brimming waters

Feeding ducks
there is never enough bread to go round
on Saturday none left in bakeries
not even stale bread

Then there was
Christmas I happened to make a note of the fact
here on Boxing Day

Next the question is can
they proceed beyond the opacity
of their simulacrum of analytical
language and will they be able to
confront the ontological question
if it means a redirection of their
present verbal resources?

The answer is of course No however much
we admire that pugnacity of style.

Linguistic not manual as in
'Don't come those strokes with me then.'

You can say thank you the hands
are better now

Yesterday's rigours
bricking up that hole
and cementing it over
didn't aggravate the conclusion
we have no need of finger stalls

Then New Year's Eve interposed its
traditional half-remembered ditties in the Bar till One
nothing modern ladies and gentlemen
in this House tonight
though the songs were this year's earlier on
fossil declarative style in
easy melody and forgotten words

Then at three o'clock I burnt my hair on the gas jet
failing to relight a cigar butt
natural gas flares
up ashen matted
tackiness flakes off

in a bed made for one two
get up the worse for rest
go back the way they entered

past the former gasworks
and over the marsh
a couple of anxious sphinxes

and then a visit and then another
and goodbye goodbye it's
not so far you know

I think you must enjoy this sudden
imposition of work at dusk
despite an inconsiderate delivery
half an hour before the lights switch off
which has to be arranged at once
on this traditional display stand

the clenched emotions line the kerb
hurrying off into shared privacy
like plastic poppers on a
quite ungraded necklet
the very order of benches on a
pay as you enter bus
stopped at traffic lights
its rigid passengers the only
illumination down the entire street
unembarrassed yet like involuntary
reflections sharing one idea
with the other candid customers

This will do and so I walk to
collect my purchase at the off-licence

Yes it is peaceful

Most peaceful last of years

That laurel that is not a bay
over there it
sways a lot

Why not a whole bush?

That's going to be strong
down there

Lightly fading home to eternity
deep blue sky and darker clouds
for a few lasting minutes before
all the lights begin to come on
and I put dinner in the oven

Tomorrow not blue
pink
verging on something else but then I lost it
fleeting

Rain totally insistent drizzles
as I walk downhill over the river
back across the new bridge
down by the river walk
where it smells of malt
under an arch where water rattles in
droplets on different kinds of metal
uphill once more and left down
the walled path past the meeting house
then right and up the same hill
another way step inside and out
after two pints into
pelting rain drenching for
200 yards to our house
out of my coat and shoes
sausages in fridge, oranges in bowl
where has this tin full of biscuits
come from?
reading and dozing on the couch
till the phone rings

dreaming of being awake
it's Jean at another station and
Goodness! it's Six already
a few biscuits in a paper bag
slip on my dry shoes
and twenty minutes to what
seems like an assignation
at the Bridge
a quick drink and
take her home
from work after dinner
we split a can of brown ale
and she falls asleep

Brought down my cart of bricks
painted doors and fanlight windows

dusted, polished, rearranged
Grandad's bright colours and now
quiet care with equal care I
rearrange each piece in its drawer
the way I remember it the
handle gone but how strange it is
painted Andrew T. K. Crozier
& Co Ltd Builders and
Contractors Phone 824
while I remember it as Knights
in yellow lettering and black dimensional
shading
               offcuts fashioned to a chip
off an old block if I rolled
a barrel of blazing tar down that
hill I'd be put away

But such stories persist
like something left behind just as you go through the door
not slowly perceptibly fading but suddenly
just the news of a totally new set

If turning back opened up
alternatives I assert with confidence
you would not have existed
so lacking comparison
variety is real

Revealing what there was or
it can be said to represent
what is missing

The car starts this morning without choke
the battery is dry the plates warped
gaping to be filled

No heavy duty sacks
Next there will be no polythene
Palimpsest

Find a use for these things
renew and reuse

Closing the attic door on memory
and bringing it down here
with me
                    the miniature wagon like nothing else
but a tender (dragged behind) stands
on the floor looking old-fashioned

one cube on my shelf each
face a different colour
from a choice of six
yellow red silver gold blue black

Notes de travail   Tressell

    Saw horse   Grandfather

a table in fact a strip of asbestos
18 inches from the end of a sheet

it cuts better wet
the short saw springs from the groove

two white doors

Much rain the wind blew off
my cap turned Jean's umbrella
inside out

A starling flying hard past the window
beak full of bread

Ducks
uninterested at first
bread brought home for another day

Moving on not moving in
today like an extra clarity
love refracted our presences
walking down the street
into the rain still there
an after-image of complement
bodily hypnagogic we were
two but the memory is one

Asleep upstairs
the bedclothes tuck in your body heat
draughts eddy the curtains not a breath
can insinuate down your back

Poem of this Poem

The landing light through our bedroom door
fixes your posture. I create darkness
and enter closing the door behind me
and round the bed skirting the wall
where the window faintly implies spaces
more than I feel. Undressing into the cold
with an apprehension of warmth in

regular low sounds an interval which is
continuous and repetitive as I fall
beneath the bedclothes and roll over
to my side engaging your outline and
rest. Balanced. You return to sleep
diffusing heat and moisture. The other
person I sleep with I am as ever
beside you drawn into the breaths
you take. Not speaking. Hearing such space
that slowly stills into an ambient
jointure of being. Here. Far off.
The world rises into us

Perched in a pear tree the starling's
puny song barely penetrates rather
it preens and fans its insignificant wing

light speckles its radiant plumage
glossily colouring where today
is dulled

The ducks aren't hungry but
sit on the island
stirring occasionally

A pair of jackdaws, or maybe rooks, but
I'm sure jackdaws appear and warm themselves
against that chimney stack
smoke on the wind winds over them
as they flex precariously against
the bricks ready now to fly
one after the other off
across the cutting

Rarely able to sense the pregnancy of cosmos
these days I make a number of local compacts
veiled in desire for whole ground
the non-reductive

smoke from the same chimney and a garden fire
matter rising to its final state
turning along the wind and dispersing
out of sight
no image that I can grasp
more than I hope to
the fires are invisible
tightening painfully on the body to release
the heat rising towards its source
clouds mantle the world's radiance
rain falls in straight off the sea
and gleams on the pavement
inaudible creeping edge
staining each step

False Spring
was my muse for all this refusal of damage
as the heart rises in unlooked for sunlight
to the frantic activity of animals
within their world
behind the hedgerows

imperceptibly then it is almost over
not false but not authentic either
unlike the punctuation of night

In torchlight to know where you are
and then switch the beam off
to catch a glow at the heart of the fire
charred open at the top
but settling into itself
burning slowly to leave
scarcely any ash

flames interrupt darkness
dried out at inevitable flash point
sparks rise into the air above my head
until they extinguish no longer sparks

I am out to damp the heap down
and it's pre-dawn
                                        birds all at once
cut through the air calling out

steam rises off the crying cinders
grey enough to see

but I am unused to this crispness
in the world and walk around the garden
wide awake in space

Colourless like the offering light
the world returns in primary quality
distinct as afternoon but not for me

Needing to wake up yet still dreaming
I return to the house where Jean waits for me sleeping

the horizon is a veil towards which I adapt
in acknowledgement of the sun
about to rise over the houses

the cool air stirs indoors and
the blinds flap at the open window
light pleating through on the floor

i.m. Rolf Dieter Brinkmann

Already the ducklings resemble their aunts and uncles
free of all obvious maternal bond
the brood moves in and out of itself
involuted and explosively bobbing
in each other's wake

their movement appears haphazard
and even elegantly natural they all
look the same and know what they want

when we appear under the shadowy leaves
with our bags of bread

it is a sign for them to
come to the edge and when it stops
and the last crumbs are shaken out
into the dirty water they move off
together again while you and I

set off round the pond talking
about ducks and the volume of foliage
on a summer branch which dips
toward the water to be reflected
in words that condense like the image

of each leaf shifting over the others
while unreflected light flickers through
in a web of shining brevity
that glows all night long
as air moves and water rises

within those immense columns
echoing: all language is truth
though a bed of dry leaves when evaporation
ceases and our words turn and fall
flickering with our life upon the earth

-o0o-

Duets *was published in 1976 by Circle Press Publications, Guildford, in an edition of 150 copies with an original lithograph by Ian Tyson.*

-o0o-

Duets

for Ian Tyson

Punctual as returning something
now worn-out winding back
the tension in a spring
which daily use makes slack

Passed by familiar straight lines
on an array of worn-out topics
to agree to a manual of signs
at which abruptly the point sticks

Stemming back from its confluence
the topic hovers upon the air
turned inside-out in a display of patience
surrounded by ravels that hold it there

The ink flows from the cartridge
like tracer hovering in the path
it swerves across time like a bridge
to the future emptying from its bath

Level to the horizon
the jagged peaks trace beneath the star
which these telescopes imprison
like supine distance dragging on too far

Without stopping the axis turns
across the ground quite jaggedly
and goes on turning and never learns
the ground is lying flat and peacefully

Now the word quickly moves forward
tight and unrelaxed across the heart
within a confined space like Mother Hubbard
poor little dog it is time for you to part

Music perhaps this time round
heartily itself like a two-year-old
playing on its own without a sound
from what its sticky fingers hold

Bowed down by the weight of care
while in the garden on last year's buddleia
butterflies hover in the purple air
something is subsiding slowly into fear

Speak for this gentle creature
on the garden path and say its name
aloud to graft its finest feature
in your mind for you're the same

Perhaps a stroke would change it all
say for the better but maybe for the worse
an angularity from which the points fall
into dull rotundity like an empty purse

Fervent desire meshed with
sheepish sorrow but administ-
ering a commonplace come hith-
er look of imagine what you've missed

Clouds tug across the pane of blue
like sheep struggling at a gate
barred to them which they must pass through
or stay there quite abandoned to their fate

The shadow acknowledges the sun
happily in step like the body it follows
until it is swept up by clouds that run
across the sky nearly coming to blows

Not the same place twice
unlike the well-turned rhyme
easily used unlike dice
no lightning will strike this time

A Long Story But Not a Tall One

Richard Long set out to walk a line
turning it at right angles to make a square
and found it made a triangle an obvious sign
that where you start from is no longer there

Honey from onions onion round an egg
so sweetly right and latticed in the wax
of first impressions they could scarcely beg
a higher finish hanging there on racks

A spiral like a crab in the sand
washed up and dragged round in a spin
of tracks melted in the ooze and
fading out of life so brief and thin

Loosely dragged through wet snow
which rusts round the runners like nests
in a refurbished rookery all set to go
in a rush over the hill where the sun crests

Four ducks fly over a low road
running hidden by branches and the rain
they shed from their wings has slowed
to the rustle of leaves in a dry drain

Down is the same for warmth or laid
beside the head hides the longest way
round between two points quickly made
in a bed of earth to close the day

As though the air at rest is still
beaten by wings that at length have stirred
but almost hears the launching thrash and mill
of pinions streaming round the feeding bird

Such dizzy roots coil like skywriting
then stir away from the web as
emergent runners no longer short of airing
room gradually turn green beneath the gas

Now everything is upside down and insects
cast their shadows in this quarter
like light itself as it reflects
a water droplet in a drop of water

It can't be anything like sibling
likeness that has massed these lines lost in
rivalry for which one is looping
around the other like loose folds of skin

The ornaments confuse the grammar
stuffed like an aubergine and lost for
ever with a hopeless snarl of denture
polish and yet dare to ask for more

The dialectic expires on its feet
four stuffy corners superimposed
and unable to budge even to greet
the future imperfect that had never closed

Short and thin or long and curly lines
with two cast-off kinds of ending
pair off like opposites whose nature inclines
to covert types of correspondent blending

The golden section spirals growing to
be always the same two ends of crêpe
on something else a little heap of goo
within for its particular shape

Leaf tremor for a passing train
faint as a song-thrush always in the mist
in which a fox lingers like a stain
about to disappear on lips that kissed

-o0o-

In an interview with Andrew Duncan, published in Don't Start Me Talking, *Crozier explained some of the background to the writing of the volume* High Zero, *published by Street Editions in 1978. Duncan asked Crozier to 'talk us through its structure' and suggested that the title referred to* High Pink on Chrome *by Jeremy Prynne and* Striking the Pavilion of Zero *by John James. Crozier's replies are instructively precise about the nature of composition and reference.*

The two flanking poems are parodies of poems in the Prynne & James volumes respectively, repeating lines from the main block of text; however, I don't see it as a reply to them. I say 'block of text' because I think of it as a square of 24 x 24 units: the writing procedure was to start at the top and work down, i.e. first I wrote 24 first lines, then the second lines and so on. I don't know if that tells you much…

Both those books, by Prynne and James respectively, were published in 1975. *High Zero* is written according to a very simple arithmetical format whereby the number of poems is the same as the number of lines in each poem, and the poems were not written sequentially but as so many first lines, so many second lines, so many third lines and so on. I thought I would complicate that by introducing a more definite constraint whereby some of the lines, which had to sort of graft themselves on to what was there already, at the same time had to be able to fit in the context of two other poems, those poems being based in their format on the last poem in Prynne's book, which I placed first, and the first poem of James's book, which I placed last, poems which were written according to constraints I knew nothing of. And at the time I suppose I thought that the introduction of various patterns of constraint was a stimulus. But I don't think you can go beyond that to… I wouldn't go beyond that to speculate whether there's some kind of implied critique of either of the two books mentioned, or of the two poems chosen.

Duncan went on to ask about 'first-person' experience in the poem and Crozier's answer reveals an interesting comparison between High Zero *and the later poem 'Free Running Bitch':*

In one sense this poem is full of personal experience. Fragments of it rather than a narrative about it. It was written over a certain period of time, during which I was doing all sorts of usual things one does, passing from different times of the day and night, different immediate locations, different personnel, which I then turn to as the immediate context for or source of material for the next line. And it might offer some clarification if I then go on to say I chose the word material then as distinct from content, because if there is allusion for example to a night-time walk over the Downs, that doesn't then constitute that as content of the poem, and the procedure for writing the poem works against what is drawn from personal experience. Retaining that modality because it has entered what I hope is a kind of strong field of material. And other stuff altogether, such as the series of linguistic terms which poems develop as they proceed from start to finish. And part of the strength of that field is that there is an accumulated background, and part of its strength is that there is a sort of constant displacement sideways, in that the sequence of thinking about working on material that is derived from personal experience doesn't treat it cumulatively within a particular poem that makes it relevant. I mean sideways in the sense of implicating an adjacent place in the next poem which you only get to when you've turned the page, having read several more lines of the previous poem, as though it recurs with the periodicity of the poems themselves…

I would say that taking autobiography broadly, *High Zero* contains a great deal of material which might be thought of as autobiographical, although it's not actually been put together as a narrative, so if a biography means some kind of narrative about a subject, so you might want to allege, or want me to allege, that the material then ceases to be autobiographical, as a result of the kinds of pressures I've described. On the other hand, 'Free Running Bitch' is in many respects quite directly autobiographical, and yet I wouldn't feel that in the way those poems are conceived and written, that they allow for any notion of strong tension between truth-telling, by virtue of narrative, on the one

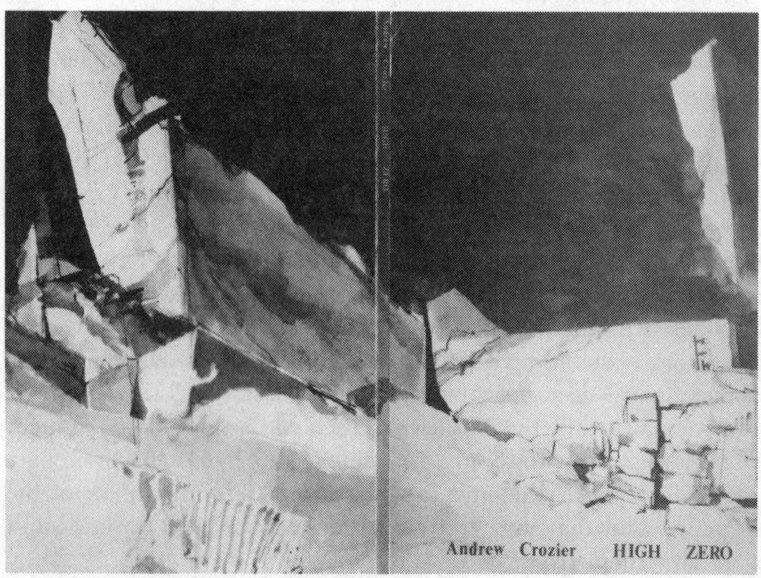

hand, and the autonomous work of art on the other. I don't think those two issues need be in tension, except when they're defined in such ways that that tension is turned into a stand-off, and they're treated as though they are mutually exclusive. Which is what I mean when I use the word stand-off. So coming back to the question, if we're talking about modernism, then part of the background is the inescapable belated novelty of much of foundational modernism for people growing up in the 1950s and 1960s. I think the sort of modernism you come across depends very much on your social circumstances. For example, those educated at universities would come across the novelty of Ezra Pound and William Carlos Williams in the early 60s, two or three generations too late; whereas others might in museums and public libraries come across other things.

Duncan:
The original edition of *High Zero* has got a painting of a Carrara marble quarry. Does that shed light on the poem?

Crozier:
It's a very large monochrome wash drawing of quarries by Ian Potts who is a Lewes-based painter and a friend of mine, and he produced a large number of such drawings in the mid 70s, of various sizes. They're monochrome, which is not strictly typical of his painting, in order to represent the very high contrast of black and white in the quarries under the Mediterranean sunlight, reflected light and shadow. And as well as the rather impenetrable shadows there are a whole series of reflective surfaces which are variously rubble, stacks of marble waiting to be sold on to sculptors and other consumers, and there are a number of places in the poem where my looking at these drawings is part of that experience of everyday life we discussed earlier, and drawn upon thus. So talking about light falling upon things, which I think goes on throughout the poems, may be about daylight, dawnlight, if you like, light as experienced within the diurnal cycle. So you get your cycle in that way. But it's also about the experience of looking at and reading Ian Potts's transcription of a very different quality of light, in particular the way that perhaps engages with a certain content as represented by the rubble or blocks, which the light articulates just as much as does the shadow. The drawing actually reproduced on the cover wasn't chosen particularly for what it represented so much as it could be

bled off at the edges to yield an image which would fit the format of the dustwrapper. Nobody else illustrates that… the kind of thing I'm talking about, but perhaps not as forcefully as some of the other drawings in a more conventional, less landscape format, although of course actually as folded around the book they're not landscape format at all.

Duncan:
The procedures which allowed you to build *High Zero* are the key information not printed in the book. It's not that people would want a volume of Collected Procedures, but I'm curious to know more about how you devised such a procedure, and other procedures you used, because I think a lot of people are unfamiliar with this approach to writing.

Crozier:
It should be self-apparent that the number of poems and the number of lines per poem are the same. Although that doesn't then lead to understanding of the actual sequence of the writing, it should suggest that there is a relationship between the two. I very easily see that relationship as being rather like that of a grid on a square format, in which the number of divisions on each side is the same, not unlike a square on an Ordnance Survey map, for example. It's also, I think, self-apparent that the first and last poems in the book, which are different in shape to the other poems, stand outside that format, while nevertheless having all their lines repeated, or recurrent, within the poems that make up that format. So both of these features of the writing, it seems to me, are completely overt, and provide strong clues to something about the character of the writing as conceived or as intended. Anyone reading the book at the time might quite reasonably have also been expected to have read books by Prynne and James so that although there's no direction, other than a kind of hint in the title *High Zero*, to specific books, there's a reasonable expectation that that kind of dragging one's coat-tails, let's say, will be picked up on, as it appears to have been picked up on at least by Grimly Castafiore. And of course also there's the dedication of the book to Prynne and James. Therefore I think I can say that the features of the writing and the way they contribute to a reading of the poem, are fully candid, certainly for the readers I was able to envisage at the time. Then of course anyone can come along and say, are these things actually exhaustively true? And certainly there was a problem at one point, in sending the manuscript round,

when I lost a line from one of the poems, and there's one of the poems which visually on the page looks much more erratic in its disposition than the norm. And it would I think be quite apt to ask, 'was this written in quite the same way as the rest'? To which the answer must be, 'No, it's an erased poem'... Or what's left after a certain amount of erasure.

Duncan:
It's hard to look at it without having a kind of shimmer of a different text it's made out of.

Crozier:
Yes, I think that's why I left the words disposed on the page as they had been previously, that's the trace of before. There's a point we haven't touched on at all which we should touch on, which is that these poems...the way the group of poems is set up as a formal object recurrently involves drawing attention to the significance of the line, to the line of verse as a unit, and to the line of verse as a unit which can perform different roles in different contexts. Leaving aside the question of lines of verse as things which can perform different roles in different semantic contexts, which is something which individual words are also required to perform, I think very important to understanding something about my poetry is the attention I pay to lines as units of composition, and relations between one line, and the preceding line, and the next. And that raises inevitably the topic, it seems to me, of what is referred to variously as metre or metric or prosody or rhythm or measure. Those matters which are if you like a component in the technical material of poetry as a medium. I don't think I go as far here in ensuring or attaining a kind of absolute autonomy for individual lines as I do in a later poem called 'Humiliation in its Disguises', in which each line could stand in isolation as a kind of caption although the way they're put together brings out a kind of syntax running through the poem as a whole.

Duncan:
It could foreground the act of combination as well as disjunction?

Crozier:
It seems to me one of the most interesting things about poetic language is its conjunction of bringing together of larger or smaller units. Or bringing together of elements into smaller and larger units.

Thus drawing attention away from the largest unit as the ultimate verification of what meaning may be, which I think is one of the things which a notion of full and complete utterance or a bit of a sentence or a bit of sententiousness or an intended communication falls short of, overlooks. I hope you can put that back together as a sentence.

Duncan:
So these are the units which are to be disposed and the field is the way in which they can be disposed? A set of relationships which they are going to enter into?

Crozier:
I would probably think that having demonstrated that a line can be repeated in a different context and remain integrally itself and at the same time have its weight and significance affected by a different context, that it ought to be possible to go on doing that indefinitely with any particular line. And if a line on the one hand is unique in itself and at the same time not unique in its context, then the other possible contexts in which it might play a functional role rather than remaining true to itself ought to be thought of as indefinite, without a theoretical limit to the number of possibilities.

Duncan:
So the 24 poems point to a much larger, even indefinite, set of possibilities, which they're a sample from?

Crozier:
Treating the book as something read from cover to cover, then the reader's experience would presumably be: read the first outlying poem, go on to read the main block of poems and have an experience of déjà vu, and then read the second, closing outlying poem and have recurrent senses of déjà vu throughout, since all those lines would have been encountered already.

Duncan:
They might pick it up and they might not. Is it a motet where one systematically… A catch, or a round…

Crozier:
I think a musician would probably pick that up much better. I don't think music enters into my calculations here. I probably have a very

naïve set of understandings about music which would regard it as wild and novel. Not subject to artifice of the sort I've been describing. Which I know is perfectly opposed to the case of music, but nevertheless my experience of music tends to ignore the fact. Which means I'm not a skilled listener.

Duncan:
I'm a bit surprised, because Zukofsky and Bunting were so preoccupied with music that…

Crozier:
Indeed, and, when I was initially formulating ideas about the poetry of my epoch with a view to carrying on post-graduate work, it was in terms of the analogy between poetry and music, because that was so strongly solicited by amongst others William Carlos Williams in his later writings on measure, quantitative verse – but I came to the conclusion that what one was dealing with was at best an analogy rather than a strong structural identity. Partly because, as I've increasingly come to think, poetry is something which is read rather than heard. I think that's the condition in which we experience poetry, certainly the condition in which I experience poetry, although I can in reading it put, imagine, it in the context of being voiced, I can read it aloud, or I can read it inwardly, obviously that seems to me an incidental material enrichment rather than something which contributes to either the poetical form or the poetic significance. Which might seem to beg the question, What can I possibly mean by talking about prosody? It means I still think that there are formal features associated with language's material qualities which are the basis of rhythm. And I don't think performance is necessarily a very good guide to anything other than the rhythm of the performance. Certainly not to the sort of authentic rhythm within a good text.

Duncan:
I think a performance is a social event, and the people in the room compose a large part of the meaning of the event, rather than just the text. It would be a bit paradoxical to argue that they're simply amplifying it. It's hard to believe that.

Crozier:
It used to be frequently alleged in the 60s and 70s, and no doubt subsequently, that by hearing poets read their work a reader attained

to a much clearer and authentic understanding of the rhythmical character or signature of the text. Which I don't think could possibly be true. Many poets are very bad readers, and bad reading can have all kinds of qualities, including too strong a commitment to sounding good, and even contradict what one might think was the evidence of the written page in front of one, as in comparing the two by following the score at a concert. So I think that that whole line from Pound's early insistence that the separation of word from music led to poetic degeneracy, down to Bunting's reiteration that the pleasure of poetry was in the sound, not the words, is unhelpful, certainly unhelpful to me, and I don't think it stands up to scrutiny when looking at the work of either. And I think since you mention Zukofsky that, although he may have had both a kind of, I want to say spectrum, but I should probably say ratio, that runs through speech as a lower limit to music as an upper limit, and although he has described several of his poems, the shorter ones, as songs, and he has talked about *'A'* as the equivalent to Bach's St Matthew Passion, he's also – I don't know whether it was Zukofsky or someone else, perhaps James Laughlin, described *'A'* as an epic of the class struggle. And Zukofsky's whole tendency as a poet seems to me to be towards the semantics of the lowest semantic function of language, by which I mean the semantics of enunciation and audition. I don't think that can be equated with music. I think that's there in his Catullus translations, it's there in late poems like '80 Flowers'. Anyway, let's not pursue that, because I haven't thought my views through entirely in relation to Zukofsky.

I've introduced the point about the line, which seems to me to follow from the account I initially gave of *High Zero*, because I suppose I thought of myself throughout as a poet whose practice has been led by thinking about prosody generally and prosodic decisions locally, on the assumption that those things are the irreducible identity of poetry, and that this in turn means that my range of tolerances when reading poetry is tested when I fail to discern the presence of other prosodic effects or prosodic decisions, so that I am at a loss to recognise where the language is coming from, because it comes from those matters in the first place.

-oOo-

High Zero

For John James and J.H. Prynne

While the grass spoils underfoot
like glass, the sound sharp and clear,
frost persists in the air while the sun rises,
looking 'as if it were a lamp of earthly flame'.

But at the surface, like a separate place
the picture of this is over-exposed. But
in shock, rare gases leave their stain to
burn its bright sign on everything.

It would flout its law: saturation by
the contents spread anecdotally (BAL).
Shored up together to breathe
you hear the brain stay tuned to you.

The evolution of the principle optic
content is an illusion. So much
like marble in sunlight. The grain
is true or stained with loss.

And for ever and a day runs on
at arm's length, held with scents
too vivid to see: beneath
the reckless apex of that hope.

A pleasure shared
                    at both ends of a string
    hands oppose the work of teeth
until both unclench their grip on
condition all but nothing in the room
any longer recalls the hypotenuse
it sags and upon our feet again
hover before the onset of 'Ennui'.
                        Like angels turning our backs
                                        to heed the call
of fallen comrades

                          and fall on top of them.
Shored up together to breathe
the fumes of evening
gathered in an airless room
its windows still warm to touch
are tinged with pink
reflections of faces like
stray atoms in a chaos
trying to better themselves
and liquefying painfully. The gases
rarefy towards the ceiling
heated in the light
that sets them off.

Crumpled beside yesterday
    it is a dream before birth
before the company is brought together
and the reunion commences.

Isn't this the shirt you wore?
It is time's memorial
    like a favourite colour
that no longer moves you

until you pass somebody else
in an adjacent register
and your tone noticeably changes
    in a painful seizure

    that wears you out.
Being the same size helps
but the standard remains the same
until the commencement of business

one day brings with it a complete
conversion of the measure
    everyone took for granted.
The same quantity carries forward

they claim, hopefully, new style:
    bear it in mind
for being generously impartial
you too can don the uniform.

Run into a sodden blur
of lamplight on the pavement
– as though no cracks yawned
except where children walk –
the air is heavy with mist
flat out like condensation on a window.
Surface tension vs. gravity.
It would flout its law: saturation by
an abrupt inversion of evaporation
precipitate hotness in the clammy dark.
If you can remember the sun
and make the appropriate local adjustment
its rays will fall precisely
at your feet like natural flame
to consume your thoughts.
Dry to any reflection
the burnished metal of your head
seems to repel the sunlight
by staying indoors, just before
dawn you go outside and the dew runs
from your forehead like sweat
which you wipe from your upper lip
in a conditioned reflex
action like a child.

The advance of happiness
is never an anniversary
nor as the evening light fades
once more and shadows disappear
into the world of objects
should one think of a return
for the light is given back
from its destination and absorbs
the atmosphere of a curtained room

within its swift recoil
and it is abruptly dark indoors
while every rambling rose gleams
like blemished skin in a cleavage
even now last night and tonight
border on resemblance
like the natural twins of an impeccable
bloodline the stock reverts
around them fruitlessly
and uniform like something gone
from memory the date not written
down and the day unobserved
for good slipping past
like thieves of time
escaping to the wilderness.

The stems are covered

Round them the water disappears
bluer and heavier than air
which is silvered at the surfaces
of small bubbles clustered to them

But at the surface, like a separate place
the blue is the solution
of reflected light in glass
on which repose highlights
sinking along the side of the bowl
in which the colour of the flowers
and the reflected colour of the air
wait to be wiped dry

As they're lifted out with a sponge
oil floats away from the water
in indifferent repulsion
the differentia of like from like

Out of the medium floats
the shadowed lightness of a branch
crooked with aged growth

the colours fade and harden
exposed to too much sunlight
still they adhere to the flowers
and leaves they skilfully attend.

All of your ideas
                    begin life again
when you wake up
    your faithful servants, already at work
    in their accustomed places
like clothes neatly folded on the chair
which no one else could wear
in quite your way, grown fat
on the success of small ambitions
which you dream about
and can't outgrow
like permanent convalescence
there's no escaping them.
The way your friends remember you
clips over like paper
cut to fit a larger model
they never seem to change
the way you do, their thoughts
were your thoughts, and they note
your points like rival connoisseurs.
Drop a coin into the slot
and a kind of truth comes out
I SPEAK YOUR MIND
one foot cheating on the ground.

Then in the smoke
                the extinction of light
whatever follows is masked
by tears that smart the eyes
like blurrings of hot fat:
the picture of this is over-exposed. But
from its opaque depth there emerges
a counterfeit sadness

tender as regret, wet
as undried tears
a little smudged and reddened
a little rubbed-in message
that'll teach you. The darkness lifts
towards the horizon and stops
at the water's edge
in its deepest tone, over the rim
where all at once the sky lightens
perceptibly out of touch
like a disappearing vessel
dipping its flag conveniently,
Farewell. Whoever else
would see it quite like that
so empty just the place
to sink in out of sight.

All that it should be
the night long white
glow of insomnia upon glass

cloudlike as the brain where it meets
the narrow band of light clear as dust
in the eye the material world dilates

in shock, rare gases leave their stain to
register that brief catastrophe
across the stomach wall

no other aftermath
a path to the downstairs door
by way of the kitchen window

where the animals all come in
to feed in turn, nudging their plates
over the vinolay in silence

no less heavy than their sleep
and just as fugitive their days
go haunting the neighbours' gardens

animating the shadowless grass
which gleams by night in parched
neglect just covering the earth

like a tattered quilt and
patched with weeds it barely
holds the heat of the day.

In the time it takes
a beak to probe a grass's root
or a heart-beat to lose its echo
within the automatic illusion of memory
like glass, the sound sharp and clear,
too brilliant to the touch: within
the body cavity: unequal pressure
across the surfaces keeps up
the polished moment with its smears
of iridescent after-image, not quite forgotten
meals which cost too much,
a quick wipe over the formica with a damp cloth
and all's forgotten in a moment
when the breasts tilt this way
beneath her butcher's apron
adding another ten per cent
finally to level everything out
in a discreet eructation
and the instant's past again
the interrupted sounds resume
the hour in compact ratio
of undeleted silence, added
in the inventory it augments
the average of successful song.

Where did such sound come from
                                        high heels on metal
receding over stone
                    before the circuits close again
potential at the furthest ebb

gone down
            where it excludes itself.
The street dips to the left
until the lamplit haloes wane
and something follows in ensuing darkness
in the endless fading echo where
long after the machine's gone dead
you hear the brain stay tuned to you.
What would you lose?
The echo of an echo
in fugitive half-life
looped into itself until
the erasure made itself heard
over the message. Forgotten
noises clamour for attention
first thing in the morning
seeking another time zone
to transfer to before
you recollect their source.

Rain drips in the casement
                    of an outdoor life
            from day to day bonheur
where condensation clings as though breath
would fly through the window
            still moving slowly
in a gathering wave at the meniscus
      ready to launch itself
in immaculate newness.
                        It ripples slowly down
the reeded glass like igniting neon
its reluctance suddenly overcome
before the air can soak it from
the surface down into the lungs
it begins to flow
directly in a current with flat
orderly movement. Beneath
the cill its cruel overflow
picked out in evidence
from the dirt where drops heavily

fell has annulled that contract.
Add your name to the glass
through which you witnessed this
time soon mists over it.

The cat washes audibly
and yawns at four walls
snorting and sharply rigorous
for a moment in its search
then discards like knitting
when numbers drop from
the sum no longer a true count
and everything can start over
in another place. Next door
plates of half-eaten food on the floor
wait to be cleared away
all day if you'd like the job
you have to crawl on hands and knees
to pick them up. In the sink
dried particles soak off and float
free under the surface heavy
with further saturation.
Scales dry on your fingers
next like blistered skin
they lift off like a casual symptom
you get used to overnight.
Then you can start again
keeping the animal amused for
a while back where you started.

Let it begin again
hopeful as a glance of recognition
at the end of a line
                    Isn't this where
frost persists in the air while the sun rises
and the light seems to dawdle
as though it was already a late morning
and the windows were opened
      the rooms airing nicely

the linen we brought tossed over the foot of the bed
in a jumble of healthy intention
If you fold the corners like this
you'll sleep more comfortably tonight
the look tired and meaningless
but the edges all straightened out
                    Weren't you there
in the valley when the sun set
and the mist crept inland
like a discarded band of crêpe
the windows lighting up in ones and twos
   the rooms all taken
the luggage unpacked into drawers
most of it brand new and unmarked
if you follow metonymy.

A cloudy night
                    lit from beneath
for this is earth-shine
and whatever comes between us
is permeable to our will

And see, spread in that colourless glass
the double image of the garden trees
jerks like an optical toy
you point at the sky
as though the horizon

And you are half-asleep and see less
through such an instrument than while you pointed it

The evolution of the principle optic
fibre is far from complete, we know
enough to admit as much, but
prediction is tentative. You see
intermittently through silhouettes
of trees to where across the valley
the darkness relieved along the crests
of the next hills is streaked
with falling stars.

Don't come any closer
than you are already
that's quite far enough.

Such feeling for symmetry is
                        in the eternal tables
where the horizon meets
the horizon in a boundary line
that surrounds us with the sky

as in a clouded retina
in which the light is like a cataract
saturated with atmosphere
until it spills with emotion
                        like a paper bag

                        covered with advertisements
which its contents render illegible because
content is an illusion. So much
that can't be looked into
in these holiday transparencies

with their lack of foreground
and focus set to infinity
as though it was a wall
                        run up by the shutter
timed to the split second

in which the sky tilts away
as the light decelerates to 0
                        on a soft surface
spread for such emergencies.

Another tarmac scab
under the grey lake which wrinkles:
the great skin of water
closed by the old wound of the moon.
Like a broken path to the horizon
the world is in braille

and enlarged accordingly
until its brilliance is dimmed
into the tactile surrounds
of an auditory tightrope
the yawning sea of fallen expectation
now the object is bright and opaque
like marble in sunlight. The grain
runs through the mountain to emerge
running at its foot in the surf
which foams in fragments heaped up
like beds of rubble. Halfway along
only the air is visible
and frightful, not half fast enough
for anything but a low-pitched green
blur no further off
than it looks. Black out
in either direction
and fall like Icarus.

Light is in the curtains
like a bright veil of numbers
that rises in folds over and over
and the calculus of persistence
undogmatic and fluent in its changes
draws back with the weave
its light released
in a white rinse.
                                        Shaken out
like sparks from a bed of embers
dimmer and dimmer to the touch
but there to be drawn back
the shadows fall into the room.

And for ever and a day runs on
without resistance, turned
to a dead stop without a shudder
and starting again without pause
the world takes it all back
reversed.
                Overhead the gears seemed

for ever about to slip
under the strain they bore
but the tension was maintained
in all that measured track of time.

It is
the one after
            becomes
      an accomplishment
not refused

   it is expected
your turn   will come
                             if
late still
you thought

                     this time
                  can be
             understood
               another rung
               of the sublime

too vivid to see: beneath
                        is less
                  and far from
                     underfoot
the skin

is the margin
         which decides
             you
      from now on.

Stones, leaves, broken blossoms
drift from all the seasons
here beneath the misty bushes
all laid up as if winter

was anything but a time of separation
within the edges of an all-over sky
which shrinks down to the horizon
and rather a rich hoard of unreluctant
souvenirs of other weathers
from which to select a fragment
your happiness needs just such a moment
to disclose the earth as if a cloud
is true or stained with loss.
Dew creeps along the filaments
towards the gathering centre
and unable to support itself
at last falls from the web
like recorded sound to fill
a place in the archive, spreading
its softening touch beneath
everything else, down to the root
of the matter like an axiom
that's always so reliable
there's a cue to use it.

The scenario of lies
dresses up to kill
and the leaves drift into heaps
while the grass spoils underfoot
like last year's snow
in congealed pellets of green mud
honestly you wipe your feet
on the guest mat and feel 'Welcome'
ascend through the leather like an
artful ray of hope. Oh no
the contents spread anecdotally (BAL)
and cure you of all that, what?
It just wants discipline O'Grady says.
Done with all that pass on
down the line of withered plants
and take a leaf from every other one
they're overdosed with Paris green
past any joke. Even the blue
is hard to pin a name to

preferring to describe an empty
sky in French. Sublime.
The air is choked with metal
and looks like watered silk
rolled out over heaven.

There they were surrounded
        by their infidelities
waiting to be catalogued and indexed
in the list of recurrent solutions
to problems of the modern world
some for the fourth and fifth times.

Afterwards they return home
some on buses, others by train
or car and go to bed by
twelve and at once turn off the light
to dream in innocence, the keys
to their fear among the small change
and other bits and pieces emptied
from their pockets like guilt.

Their nudity is a dirty joke
the reckless apex of that hope.

They dream of noble landscapes
and a savage truth and get
up dressed and ready to kill
for what they believe in
spite, the generous talk, of
consciousness raised like a
speculative loan
they ask for more than they can give.

Expensive dried flowers beside
your eyes in a mirror
smooth wet and dry in one light
of present accommodation

looking 'as if it were a lamp of earthly flame'.
The unfaded everlastings
and the lustre of your irises
hardly resemble one another
do they? The light expires
and with its waning flames
the metred stars go out
like flowers wrenched from the stalk.
Petals litter the carpet
and weave into the design
the hazard of their immaculate lives
settled in the dust
like ungathered nectar. The pupil
flickers in the morning light
like a black insect
dancing towards the sun
in a pattern of flowers.
The colours swarm abundantly
each has its specialist
and I am yours.

Under the umbrella
    of invisible starlight at noon
all the plants come out
    of shelter like new things
but each has a name
    given for the occasion
the visible thing it is
    a naked chance for speech
to flirt in the shrubbery
    reading all the nameplates
aromatically, by sinister touch
    a perfect stranger's sense
of decorum when abroad
    keeping the railings on the right
at arm's length, held with scents
    not straying from the path
and keeping off the grass
    which needs no label
for its name is lawn
    opening among the trees

to let the light down
    to the lowest green thing
which colours gratefully
   all that it surrounds.

Yes that's very good
        more beautiful
and no less true
   than ever before.
       Say it again.
You cannot say it again.
Burn its bright sign on everything
it sheds a
      pallor on the afternoon
as colour disappears under the headlights
in these prints.
         This time last year
was no different
the swifts will home to their nests
like bees to the scabious
beautiful in their kind
the way we remember them.
But beyond recall
for such places to recur
the colours must each revive
in their very locations
rhyming the whole spectrum
in a retained sequence
beginning nowhere.

Begin life again
from day to day bonheur
snorting and sharply rigorous

at the end of a line
let it begin again
it is a dream before birth

The advance of happiness

-o0o-

With a cover by Ian Tyson, Were There *was published by John Welch's The Many Press in 1978. It contained poems which had been previously published in* Great Works, Iron, Lettera, Meantime, The Poetry Review, Saturday Morning, *and* Spectacular Diseases. *An earlier version of 'Sundials' was published in the catalogue for the exhibition 'Seven Contemporary Sundials' by Ian Potts at the Brighton Festival, 1975.* Utamaro Variations, *a suite of four aquatints by Ian Tyson, together with the four poems published here, was published in an edition of 30 copies by Ian Tyson Editions. The text for 'Sundials' is taken from the later publication of the series of poems in* All Where Each Is, *but the dial inscriptions have been placed at the front of each poem, as they appeared in the first edition, rather than at the beginning of the sequence, as appears in the Allardyce, Barnett volume.*

-o0o-

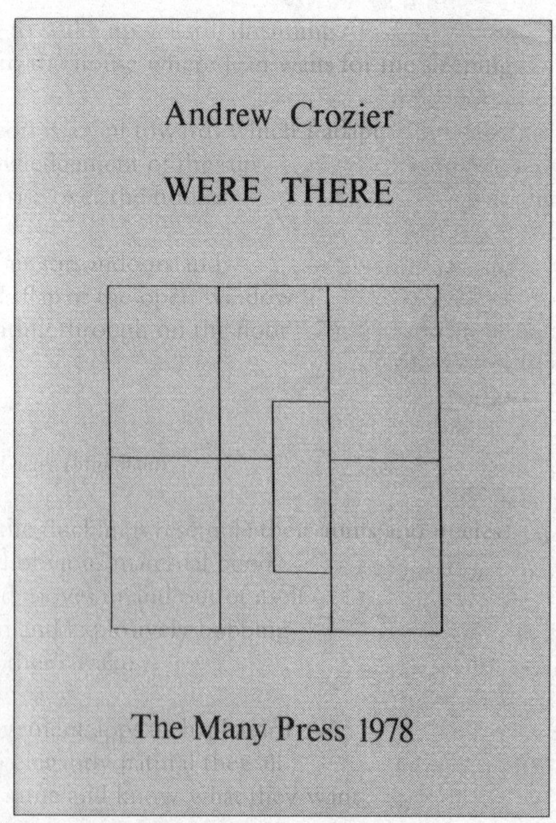

Were There

Person to Person

Nine digits and a request bring me
your answering voice within seconds but
what specifically should I say then

if feelings aren't tied to time
when but linger like general things on
trays by the bed coffee in the big one

tea in the other milk is in jug
it says time's vacuum keeping the idea
warm in blue felt pen underlining

the name you call me by before
leaving in the morning where I can
reach you still where you are now and

on your way back still moving ahead
of all speech till you march upstairs
shall I answer your call by name

Sussex Express

Any more for the fast train
passing all the small stops
more here for a Guinness

but taken from a cold tray
the unstopped throat
taking it down

the horn sounded
at the stopped cars
carrying over the fields

empty on a hot day
six white cows come on
slow enough not to stop

Sundials

For Ian Potts

1

revealed in sidereal glow we move beside the sky

Pulses with the sphere's dull shuttle
subdued by daylight
                                    against a line
its axis sheds
                    revealed
in sidereal glow
                         we move beside it
local to the sky
our feet almost lifting from the earth

2

to light a shadow in its common ground

Beats echo in the dark
thoracic cavern and emerge through
the ear of deprived sense
as thermal endurance
singular and turned to light
in constant embodiment
throwing a shadow that edges
away in its measure of
common ground

3

what lasts out its day shines in our presence

Stars lace the arteries
and veins in their fixed
places by which
a scale is set for
what lasts out its
day into another in
which their shifting
brilliance is absorbed
to warmth across the

stretched skin of
earth which shines in
our presence

4
starlight enshrines the shadows solid in their time

Light gathers at the surface
from its swift journey
while invisible slow starlight
enshrines the world into
which we emerge in
our own time to glance
passing by at the shadows
newly cast by things
slant to the sun and
solid in their time of blossom
or final rot with which
our shadows mingle equally

5
the horizon turns the earth from darkness

Inclined to the thick waves
lapping the horizon the
earth turns through them
as they recede along its other
rim unaffectible but slowly
resolved to a point among
many on the star map while
their brief outward passage
marks for the earth its
constant turning away
from further darkness

6
eyes catch up light's measure but the shadow gleams

Eyes always catching up
when light's common measure
passes at your feet
where nothing else takes

place but the idea of it
dogs your steps the shadow
finally slipping off the
plate into the future while
its luminary gleams

7

time is the shadow earth carries from us

Time is the present
still yet we watch the
shadow lengthen on the
earth which carries this
unmoving model of itself
but walk from here with
the sunrise and time shall
be with us

Local Colour

Flame rather than firelight
where the low rays focus
in dangling metal
and glance across the fields

diffuse light retreats from
the grass embedded in stubble
left closely mottled
from orange to green

the sun vanishes in a bird
scarer in the middle distance
all around the colours flatten
on to the earth like skin

Loopy Dupes

Fed back to the dot
in hoped-for recoil at this point
it weighs on the wound thread

of a button worn dangling
out of its normal rectitude
a test to tired memory
drawing its assent from the code book
where the dot abruptly refuses to budge
it is joined by others which trail behind
in meaningful suspension like a cloud
about to exhibit its other side waiting
for the stars to gleam through fixedly
their light oozing all the way
along the line blotted in a crease
which cuts the sky from edge
to edge like a sheet of paper
fresh from the quire its edges
deckled beneath the fingertips
which feel around such
flat expanse spread right across
the space it takes without pause
in its pointed dead-pan mimicry
of an act repeated in ignorance
over the pacified landscape surrounded
in speech which accelerates
constriction within the cardiac
vacuum of a tube half a size too large
for a pipe but the timetable
hums in its morning routine
and toddles in its valve like
a mute trumpet or a dogwhistle
from which some sweet adhesion on the lips
purses them despondently
as though a wilted border legume
festooned with royal imagos
gradually shrank under such attack
so moderate and in need of its spokesman
from the crazy paving to summon it
publicly and instil its virtues
in the unconscious collective able
maybe to metamorphose in the flesh
whether to transcend or sink
the submerged segments jumble
into the jammed coin slot of the drier
ready waiting to tangle

the shrunken garments which infest
those lower parts close to
the anticipated waking dream
snatched today by the sun
writhing through the glass
and curtains in a thermal aubade
administered to purge the passive
flanks of heliotrope saluting in
rank on rank led on by the left
to evaporate like haze that droops
overhead like tired pugilists
on a tour of remembrance
disliking the neat freeways
on which they speed between lights
at carefully adjusted mph
and maintained lane discipline
around the perimeter of the old town
which has been carefully restored
to the epoch of an imaginary childhood
of Easter eggs in foil
in closely guarded boxes
ready for desire unwrapped and
polished off while waiting
the nebulous crushed friables
cast off by the motor vortex
of deliquescence in the rubbery mud
which lifts like a facial mask
briefly hardened and fixed in plaster
caked on the eyes like copper
as it shrinks over the grease ready
to peel the orange off the sunset
before birds buzz ahead again
at steps through the wood and
their feathers fall like shadows or
coloured foliage in a drought
equally given for comfort or to
wear on a hat the furthest
choice is fully reconciled before
the grave is shovelled up
the wind dies down it seems
the nestlings have got round to flight
and listening expectantly for

streamers fanning through the party
air with someone's message
falling in a tangle on a lap
you bet like a novice out
for the day and slowly stifling
collapse eye to eye with an ankle
which hurries out of sight
its pair replacing it as
though sandwiched between mirrors
everything goes on diminishing like
itself like itself the recession is a
sultry war of imitation hanging
like a baggy suit of clothes
worn on the wrong occasion
suffused with sweat and flushed
around a desperate grimace or bare teeth
shining in the dark and demanding
an argument even on its last legs
trying to clamber into the ring
each foot in the way and speechless
to think of what it might do next
with just a mangled skin and no
loose ends of deceit weaving from
the cropped edges of such a brain
meant to side with its own like
an inflated stoppage which
grown into full mourning
for the child that uttered the man
on a specific genetic web
that quivered for a moment in the wake
of the earth as easing away it
left a predatory ghost to show
that exhalation fading from the glass.

Utamaro Variations

1

The colours break out and float
In the appearance of a world
Reflecting the shadows of a boat

As though an inner life unfurled
Like waves and eddying water
In a photograph its edges curled

With age while life still shorter
Yet fluent to its briefest detail
Traces its surface through another quarter

The way it passes covered without fail
Where underneath the sea in one deep note
Falls from the horizon like a veil

2

Dust coats the leaves with a sultry pallor
Impervious to shadow though shadow
Falls across a field empty of colour

Like a grid crumpled into shallow
Folds or in an unploughed field breaks
Up in the stubble like yellow

Light spread in a ragged sheet and takes
More of the earth than it does of air
Which stiff with glare and distance makes

The far-off hills seem near the bare
Chalk in the cutting meets their fuller
Slope to slide beneath the eyes' unshaded stare

3

Beneath the surface
Of clear and broken
Colours waves like lace

Fade in unwoken
Substance after all
Nothing has spoken

Forth from the wet pall
That skirts round at eye
Level like a wall

Built along the sky
Until empty space
Breaks where seagulls cry

4

The sun breaks through the leaves
In a spectral flare and edges
Their turning colours with fringed sleeves

Of smoke risen through clear ledges
In sunlight where greys seem to catch
A shape and substance it alleges

Are contained invisibly in each patch
Of shadow flickering among beams
Along the ground unable to detach

Its clearer outline from a tone which gleams
Beneath so thickened that if light deceives
Smoke ravelling a margin is what it seems

As Though After John Brett

Just out of focus
the heads of flowers occur along an edge
this side of any shadow
rejecting the presence
of anything closer
and holding the light in a blur
where colour adheres to space
and absorbs it alternately
transmitting red
white red
and the edge retreats
beneath the flowers
into the immediate rock

so that their colours
fall in a spray
across the surface
and with shadows
of birds and stone
gathered in narrow
bands of light stain and
flatten over the gradients
down to sea level
where the waves break
into the scattered whiteness
of a blank page
as though the separate colours
were not mingling
within the sober plumage
of seabirds perched along the cliff

Cardiff Docks, After Sickert

A tonal gradient edged
under the colours
covers its opaque print
with light drawn
beneath their surface
flat as any window
implied in an interior
of continuous shade
through which you might
look back to see
repeated the white reflections
of prismatic colour

Forsythia

From there across to there as though
the down-draught from a pigeon's wings
at take-off could unpleat
the limp cloths hung out to dry
on a day like this the air
divides on sunlight and the drifting
shadow of the bird outstrips the

fluttering margin of the hour
where in the angle of light and
shade across the grass
the origin and course of love pursues
and still pursues its flight

The End of a Row of Conjectural Units

Formerly the pure element
of itself, it might last forever and seem as
indistinct as the glare of the sun on a white
wall before the thought of shadows has fallen
across it; as if the flood of natural light
surfacing the bricks, the cement, and paintwork had
absorbed them all in unimpeded descent and could
keep on going : absolute space.

V
ALL WHERE EACH IS

Anthony Barnett's publishing venture, Allardyce, Barnett, had produced a collection of Jeremy Prynne's poems in 1982, and went on in 1985 to print the nearest there was to a collected edition of Crozier's poems, All Where Each Is. *Barnett's press went on to produce further volumes in this series, publishing Douglas Oliver, Veronica Forrest-Thomson, and Barnett's own collected poems,* The Resting Bell. *Towards the end of* All Where Each Is, *a title taken from a line in Charles Olson's poem 'The Distances', there is a group of poems which had not previously been published together. The first of these, 'Pretty Head', had appeared in volume 14 of* Grosseteste Review *(1981–2), and this was followed by what Crozier called simply 'Five Poems'. These are followed by a sub-section of twelve poems titled 'Half Artifice'. This last group gives a clear indication of the way he was thinking about the mysteries of both light and time.*

-o0o-

Pretty Head

1

Brought back to characteristic
Optimism in kept retreating go
Heavy on the coiled band
Tuned roughly speaking

2

A line set out of plumb
On test conditions faked memory
Looks up words in the vocab
Where a finger absolutely don't point

3

But aligns with a bunch of others
In suspense built up excess
Road to turn another over
Fixed leaves steady meant

4

Sweated light shined all
Folded over like
Paper along a dotted line
Cover from the life

5

A new line in consequence
Straight edged under thumb
Feel up all over that
Flat surface layered out

6

Space filled no vacancy
Imitated to the blankness
Obsessive behaviour patterns
A captivated appeased scenery

7

Speaks words faster
Than it tells the time
Just enough & to spare
Past a stop on schedule

8

In the opening routines
Staggered through the morning
A funnel or a whistle
Choked on adherent lips

9

Crease then in desperation
As if the earth skimmed
By perfect insect flight
Shrank gradually from attack

10

Mere need a summary
Broken slab of wide awake
Admonishment to proprieties
Together in capable ignorance

11

Different shapes of person
Either swallow or clamber over
A bloody mess of fragments mixed
In the vent hot air blocked

12

Read to stir up
The nipped in tux the vest
These lowly neighbouring parts
Expect a dream on early call

13

Shake out today backwards
Wiped off across the glass
The curtains heated chamber
Gags at emetic dawn

14

Colours of blood flow
Numb on row upon row
Dry up like condense haze
Heaven like a phrase

15

Fond memories limp
After the annual function
Vanishing ahead lights
Verge on the speed limit

16

Compliant on the forecourt
On the periphery of old
Scrupulously rendered unto
Back in a fancy childhood

17

Rapt with silver paper
Frugal but at their expense
Smoothed ready over
Come over weight downstairs

18

Absorb soluble reject
Plastic insert draw out
Power dust up
Beauty put on it face

19

Hard and to the point
Thick on the lids like brass
Greased ready to scale
Orange up to sunset

20

Migrants quiver with distance
An echo on the silence
They moult like shadows
Watered edge of sunlight

21

As much with comfort
As for the choice goes
Off face to face before
The tomb can be dug under

22

The wind would seem to drop
Ere babies start their flight
Attentive listening to
The rocket of aerial calls

23

Dressed in the message
Cut off and celebrate
Like an amateur on the loose
Day trip slow throttle

24

Drop the sights
Drawn on your eyes
A replacement like
Squeezed between mirrors

25

One steps forward two
Back we go dished
Out a hard identical
Shoddy off the peg

26

Accidents spread out
Flush to chronic pink
Embarrassed empties grin
Shining exact on black

27

But used up
Into the array
Off the words
Of what could

28

A whole skin broke
Loose ends needed trim
Chamfer round the skull
Born again mixer

29

Exaggerated in the way
Mourning suits it so well
The child admits to grow up
Family to private party

30

Hesitant a moment in pursuit
The ground draws off
Leaving too its startled ghost
Condensed its image on the glass

FIVE POEMS

Winter Intimacies 1978–1982

Street lights reflected in the wet
On the way back though the rain stopped
Before we went out
The street was empty our voices
Uninterrupted except in the silence
Between sentences
The air was thick with vapour
And almost warm we hadn't long
To keep our hands in our pockets
And step out shoulder to shoulder
Unhurried eager to arrive

And when I close my eyes I see
A vision of my choice
Light like two shadows fall towards us
Where we were
A married couple walking in the dark

Upright Captions

The cold glass
Of water mists over

The sky at night
Looks like the inside of a hole

Black coffee in a mug
With the calico print

Blue transferred
To the other side of the world

Border with Cherubs

Startled by love of hawthorn
By light of cow parsley

Twin inland sirens
Bleached on the airy fields

Revolved in the twitch of her
Goat's white inner ear

Paired doves glide and flap
Home on a withered branch

A New Compilation of Existence

Where a plate clatters
Off the terrace and enamel bowls
Rattle on the flagstones
Is the place for them

They cry in your sleep
Restless under cover of
The air you hardly breathe
And leave all this

An upturned dish with
Footprints clean away
Leaves and a few dry blades
Of grass a meal for ghosts

Or dreamers what they spare
You see swept clear as
Daylight shows you spent and
Watchful hear them go

Humiliation in its Disguises

Don't ask whose face it is when you see me
Being seen in search of your reflection

Scorched earth to the sky stopped with trees and clouds
Dumb reverie recoiled with sightless gaze
Our combat weaves through air and falls with us

Over the fluent nightfall of your rest
The costs of many bargains are exchanged
Moonlight like ice a frozen lake like sleep
Are copies made good as their replicas

The silences of portraits and dumb friends
Turn walls to margins corners sidle round
Start on arrival and shown poised to flee
Still the day lengthens colours mix and fade
A scarlet strip of empire in repose

Rooms contradict the curved weight of fatigue
Repeated details spectral and remote
Turn their straight lines from side to side and down
Where withered beauty turns its head and waits

This sacred place exposed to daily use
Shows by the flames by bare familiar trees
By recognition held back from a glance

Divisions interposed and lost in space
Darkness in layers stunned with eyes and tongues

Rise to the surface both dissolve and set

HALF ARTIFICE

Clouds and Windows

New curtains darken the room all day
Framing the glassy light of the new year

Depression wrinkles all across the map
We're in a trough, see – this shaded spot
Where the cover breaks is a screen of ice

Windows open like a gap in the clouds
On to a continent wrapped in its shrunken outline
The sky seems frozen over in a sheet
The rippled crests slow at the touch of night

Time dusts the mirror beside our bed
All movement stops at so much emptiness
Your face emerges from the depths of sleep
So suddenly I seem to catch my breath
And artificial shadows fill the air

Oh, That

The casual certainty of summer
That time's calm lapse upheld in air
And light by shadows and reflections

As if just freed of its weight
In constellations of arboreal fluff
Glimpsed and dispersed with the forward
Logic of an epoch not quite

A pattern defect repeatedly flecked
Through raw light but pinholes more
Than glints like solid specks pricked
Out in June air slow downward
Drift of filtered debris

Into corners over ledges
Bare patches under felted wraps

Evaporation of a Dream

The morning hovers in a state of panic
Terror and early fear pervade the room
Day feeds on day in starving majesty
The sky drapes heaven across the glass

Clouds drift over like strayed revellers
Fading in the light their frail procession
Crawls with lost shadows on the floor
Festoons the walls with shreds of pleasure
And peters out before it's reached the door

An atmosphere is left which dust congeals
Too thick to breathe out more than once
Cold water drops reflected as they fall

Scorn and regret condense out of the air
Earth's empty case as full as life was full

Distant Horizons

We go without a word
Not to be missed indifferent
To notice but when out of this
New splendour names in lights
Sparkle across the night

Till morning or the day breaks out
In another life like shadows

Rising against the sky
In speechless theatres
To prove us jealous of the stars

The strident audience applauds
Pleased with the way things look
While after many years
The same dumb show just still goes on

Survival Kit

The unsettled debris of the heart
Beats on steel ribs and echoes from bone

Out there the great mysterious incorporation
Moves through varieties of decay
Parts like a toppled structure
Project an architecture without foundation
Decreed in a permanent body

Here sit down in the bad air
That rattles with exhaustion
And trace the blueprint of a life

Long views of destiny cut short
At their completion date the bits
Left over fallen and falling through
Surrounding and dangerous like us

Still Life

Now shadows curved into the light again
Turn questions back like answers looking
Aside at last you see it like it is

Anywhere will do for this
Goes on all over comes out black and white
With all that fluent detail very
Clear and legibly set out one way
Or another in the negative

Like it or not it's not the same
As it appears but like itself
And was for once all one gone on
Not there but has been nowhere else

Nothing to show for this going on
No change or shadow of turning

Marble Set

Shadows eddy with reflections
Split from the mass of air and
Thickening through plane to base
Descend into the stillness of the sky

There all shapes flatten like a fallen wall
On solid depths of rock

The grain fractures at the horizon
Block struck from block in the broken dark
The intervals of stack and row
Flash in the angle of a bright façade
Steps cut across the hillside all at once

Light weathers the surface
Wearing at the edges where the stone
Closes behind its exposed face

White Launch

Thick condensation gathers on the glass
Ground soft by light that falls
From the wan moon, over the windows and the floor,
Light deepening the profoundest sleep of shade
Colder than glass it scatters in the air

No starlight surfaces
The shrunken impediment of the sky
A clear perimeter of suppression
Dried to a spectral midnight blue

Houses and trees in flattened outline
Enlarge the screen their interference fringes

The light absorbs its own reflection
Leaving no shadow of itself to shine
With colours of the world beneath its rim

Door Contre Jour

Edges start at gaps and then meet
To open and admit a wall

Say a door shut and its echo
Diverged on a straight line ah yes
From where it happens into vacant air
But doors stay put on either side
Light shrunk to nothing but a film

Too close to touch the frame
Which set new limits tilts off
Centre till the load it bears
Takes on the weight that shadows hold

Thick with the colours in which
All surfaces return passed through
A narrow band of broken white

Light Release

Clouds line the sky with a diagonal
Candour in the forehead's gradient
Each forfeiture to sleep a filtered dream

Tissue of nerves unwound in the attitude
Habit formed the corner in itself

Collateral subject of the space between
Rumpled pallor and the winding sheets
All angles in either one the grey the white
Divide repeated signals oblique stroke
Life ends and started on the other side

And air is full of a transparency
Before there start to drift the shadows
Edging across its empty surfaces
To mark a passage of unspoken hope

Fifth Variation

Round the margins invisible apertures and leaks
In barriers of retinal pigment level
Out and keep doing so while the end which is
Up goes over the side which is in

Quite like this colour on
This colour or under whichever edge
Is the edge I like them like that too

Behind it thrown in a shadow screen
Before a wall where after
Images fade in front of themselves like gaps
Closing in fog to fill an opaque gleam
The space contained is its own

The light cut in and cut out cut round
And cut back flat to reverse

Pilot Flame

Responses hasten our departure
Before each pause too short for breath
Is finished before we're ready
To start up late again we miss the cue
Too prompt to keep our rest in sight

Drag after them the way they leave
Behind their kindly light between the lines

Read this in columns and across
The numbers crowd in their allotted space
By now tomorrow's service is suspended
They say believe it on arrival

Wait here with us while the cars
File out into the traffic blocked round lights
Going our way until I'm stopped

-o0o-

The following piece of prose was published in the last issue of Grosseteste Review, *1984, and included in* All Where Each Is.

-o0o-

Driftwood and Seacoal (Family Portrait)

These men are on their feet, not all day long, when they may be on their knees or sitting on their backsides for all I know, but characteristically and most visibly they are upright, resting or in slow motion, entire and self-contained in their activity, relentlessly static. They have overcoats and caps, and the set of their heads to their shoulders, an inflexible terseness about the neck, recurring in the way the cap flattens and spreads the skull, and the overcoat's abrupt hem straightens across a stiffness behind the knee, wraps them in mistaken identity, never close enough to make apology necessary. There is something rigid between the collar bones and the scalp, between the way the knot of the tie lies against the throat and the forehead disappears beneath the headband, as though the regularity of the features is worn like an alibi. I am not where you place me. I am going down the road leading from the council estate, I am standing on the foreshore, but who you took me for must, you now realise, be miles away from where you thought you just recognised him.

What forgiveness in renewal of such error! You return as them. Stopped short again, face to face with your type, squared off from his surroundings in which I was a passer-by, I keep forgetting that you can't be here. Forgetting the vagrancy of the moment, the distances and waiting, whatever was expected, as his figure approaches, rather flat, the weight carried down the length of the spine, short legs holding the ground beneath their feet, I am out of this place, pulled together in the passage of time. Old enough, these men must be, as if belonging anywhere was now a pointless question. Why, still there of course, as long as I can remember, looking in front of them, they're like this, wherever you are. Their memories are no longer still, it shows in the hang of the coat, like a box to put things in, and the low heels of tightly knotted shoes. Years of another life, of weather in the streets and the air indoors, the hours of work, the regularity of habits, when all choices are the same, the cut of the coat, the peak of the cap, and the colour of the shoes, the size in collars, the taste in ties, the pullover and braces, determined footsteps of a steady descent, bearing it all back.

I see the difference in them, collecting from the confused after-image of wishful thinking, their presence diminished to the daily scale, going about some known business. Out for a walk will do, in these surroundings, not calling for a nod of even passing acknowledgement: people live round here. They look the same. They look out against the same earth or sea or sky, the most incommunicative of languages, speechless theatres of space, the machinery of gods. No answering back, no resonant echo, but speak for yourself. Your early history is legend, the fit of your build, the gait from the past, O never-forgotten! Those massed identities, spread one way and another, banked and scattered in new neighbourhoods. I hold them like your bearing in me, between a beacon and the showy stars, looking along the pebbles on the beach. So others in us, if, not therefore not, but also, go separately together.

VI
ON OBJECTIVISM

After having been included in the Objectivist issue of Poetry, *edited by Louis Zukofsky in 1930, Carl Rakosi's work was both rewritten and then collected in* Selected Poems. *This slim volume appeared in James*

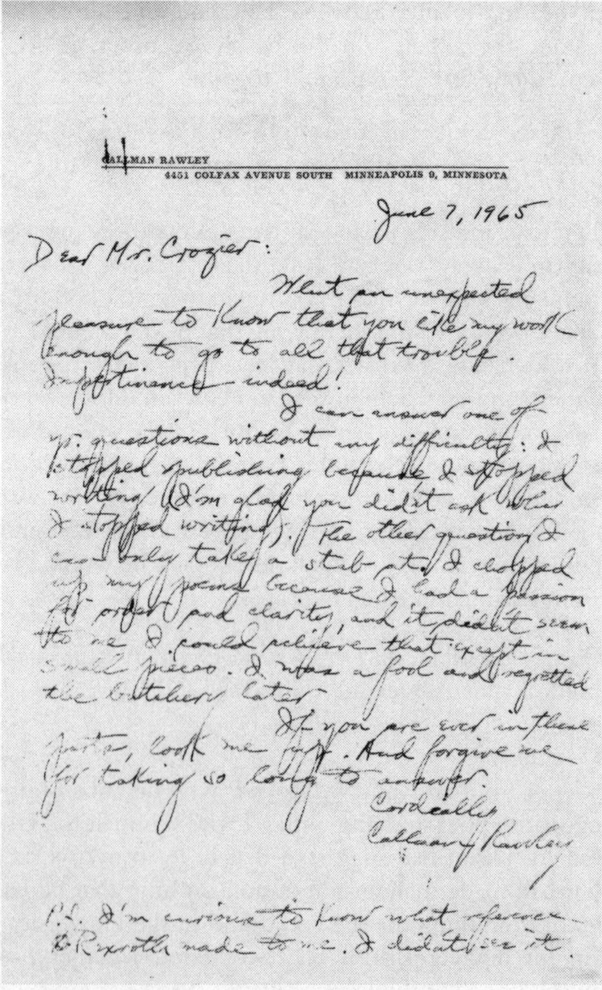

CALLMAN RAWLEY
4451 COLFAX AVENUE SOUTH MINNEAPOLIS 9, MINNESOTA

June 7, 1965

Dear Mr. Crozier:

What an unexpected pleasure to know that you like my work enough to go to all that trouble. Impertinence indeed!

I can answer one of yr. questions without any difficulty: I stopped publishing because I stopped writing (I'm glad you didn't ask why I stopped writing). The other question I can only take a stab at: I chopped up my poems because I had a passion for order and clarity, and it didn't seem to me I could achieve that except in small pieces. I was a fool and regretted the butchery later.

If you are ever in these parts, look me up. And forgive me for taking so long to answer.

Cordially,
Callman Rawley

P.S. I'm curious to know what reference Rexroth made to me. I didn't see it.

Letter from Carl Rakosi to Andrew Crozier, 7 June 1965

Laughlin's New Directions 'The Poet of the Month' series in 1941. At this point Rakosi gave up writing poetry and only reappeared in print with Amulet *(1967), which was dedicated 'To Andrew Crozier, who wrote the letter which started me writing again.' In an interview with L.S. Dembo on 4 April 1968 (published in* Contemporary Literature, *10.2) Rakosi answered the question as to what it was that had made him decide to start writing poetry again after that lapse of over two decades:*

> Well, that's a very good story. I got a letter one day that had gone the rounds of a number of different cities, before it finally reached me, from a young Englishman named Andrew Crozier. He said that he had run across my name in an article by Rexroth, had looked up my work in magazines, and copied every single poem I had written. He had made a bibliography and wanted to know whether I had written any more. Well, the thought that somebody his age could care that much for my work really touched me; after all, there were two generations between us. And that's what started me.
>
> There's an amusing bit to that letter. You know my legal name is Callman Rawley, not Carl Rakosi, and Crozier had a great deal of trouble tracking me down. Fortunately he was not discouraged by a letter from my publisher saying that he doubted if I was alive and that he had heard that I may have been a secret agent for the Comintern and died behind the Iron Curtain. However, this was only a rumour and Crozier must not breathe a word of this to anyone! I can guess where this rumour might have come from. My publisher must have gotten to someone who knew my old friend, Kenneth Fearing. Fearing and I had been roommates at the University. This is just the kind of prank he would play. I can hear him laughing like hell over it.

In a later interview with Tom Devaney and Olivier Brossard, published in The American Poetry Review, *July/August 2003, Rakosi added that he had*

> got a letter from an Andrew Crozier, who described himself as a young British poet studying with Charles Olson at the University of Buffalo. Olson had suggested that he read my work. Apparently it had made such an impression on him, that he had made copies of everything that he could find in the University Library and in his discreet British way wondered whether I was still writing. I looked at the letter. I wasn't sure I had read it right. It

was just an ordinary communication, but it was like a missive from another planet. I reread it to make sure I was reading it correctly and to collect my thoughts. I had not been with poets or given any thought to poetry for almost 25 years, so it took me a few minutes to register it in my mind. I had long assumed that nobody, I mean nobody, remembered my work any more, or even remembered my name. That Crozier found my work so interesting meant that others of his generation might also. That knowledge rushed through me and propelled me into writing again.

In 1995 Crozier edited an edition of Rakosi's Poems 1923–1941. *His introduction is a model of careful tracing of bibliographical detail and its incorporation into a thorough understanding of poetic trends. The book, published by Sun & Moon Press, won the PEN award for the best book of poetry published in that year. Geoffrey O'Brien, the editor of the Library of America, wrote to Rakosi to say that reading the collection of poems was 'like finding a new country on the map…marvelling at the freshness of what was withheld for too long. A feast of language.' The following extract is from Crozier's Editorial Introduction:*

How much of modernism went unenacted in its permanent record of published works? Not all that much, perhaps, but one important omission to note in the list of America's classic modern texts is the collection of Carl Rakosi's poems which To, Publishers, and later the Objectivist Press, intended to publish. How far Rakosi himself proceeded with this intention is open to doubt, but the prospect of collecting his work in the early 1930s was serious enough for him to have discussed with Margery Latimer, his literary confidante, the wisdom of publishing with a non-commercial imprint, and to inquire about other possible publishers. We can assume that the unpublished book would have embodied and given shape to his first decade of writing and publication at a point when he was at the zenith of his early development as a poet. We can also be certain that, although he wrote only a few more poems during the remainder of the Thirties before falling silent (the alternative was literary obscurity) for decades, in the way of other 'Objectivist' poets, the missing book would not, in significant respects, have resembled this one, although just what its difference might have been (or yet its consequences for Rakosi's subsequent career) is beyond conjecture. This edition of Rakosi's early poems cannot attempt to capture the moment of confident self-appraisal which marks a deliberate and mature first book, and is in any case sixty years too late for that. Instead it offers, without significant inflection or emphasis, the annals of Rakosi's career from 1923 to 1941.

Despite history, nevertheless, it does have something of the character of a chronologically belated first book, for what it emphatically is not is a retrospective issue of juvenilia. It is, to the contrary, a return to make good a major historical omission. Rakosi is well known now, among other things, as one of the 'Objectivist' poets, the associate of George Oppen, Charles Reznikoff and Louis Zukofsky. This group may be a construction of the late Sixties, a differentiation among the poets (including T.S. Eliot and Whittaker Chambers) who published as 'Objectivists', but it nonetheless has historical presence, and yet of the four only Rakosi is not known by his work of the 'Objectivist' epoch, which until now has been unavailable except in substantially revised forms. Thus the work on which Rakosi's historical status is predicated, as one of that distinctive group of second-generation modernists, has remained virtually unknown, in an extraordinary intra-historical lacuna. Some of Rakosi's readers will have seen his *Selected Poems* (1941) and been misled by it, for it is a valedictory gesture in which his early poems received a high-contrast treatment as cameos and vignettes; others, perhaps, will have come across some of the poems in ones and twos in contemporary anthologies or the files of old magazines. Here for the first time, however, the poems Rakosi wrote as an 'Objectivist', together with his other poems of the 1920s and 1930s, are brought together in one place in the original versions. To be able to read Rakosi thus historically is both to discover his true pedigree and to see his *Collected Poems* in the new light of its textual derivation. The reader is thus called to perform a double duty, both to attach Rakosi to the real historical past of modernism, and to reread the later Rakosi who has (no doubt partly in debt to the vicissitudes of history) been able to keep his text freely at his disposal as its own creative resource. Some readers may find that the poems collected here enable them to extend their historical understanding of Rakosi in a new and seamless unity. Others may find that the two phases of Rakosi's career remain distinct (such is my opinion) but that here at last the vigour and resourcefulness of its early phase are brought fully into view. But readers, being readers, will decide for themselves, and however that may be, here is a virtually unknown collection of original poems which, in excess of the sheer pleasure they afford, will extend significantly our knowledge of the repertoire of modernism and our historical understanding of the 'Objectivists'.

It would be inappropriate here to offer a critical appraisal of poems now for the first time seen all together, or to analyse their conditions of meaning, but it may be helpful to outline a more connected historical and biographical narrative of their production than can be provided by editorial annotation, even if only to restore to them something of their historical aura. Rakosi's career as a poet is interlocked with his life as an American: the two identities have a common dynamic and are shaped by the same historical forces. Thus if in the following account I discern distinct stages in Rakosi's early poetic career, these are also stages of assimilation and resistant self-assertion in the life of a foreign-born American citizen, whose English is the language of the external, social horizon, rather than the home, yet also the language of the autonomous self – a linguistic parenthesis around the family all the more noteworthy in a poet the epoch of whose first maturity was marked both by a strident ideological opposition of the individual and the collective, on the one hand, and on the other by a no less ideological inscription of the domestic unit as the embodiment of the American way.

[...]

If we look no further than the conflict between poetry and work, thrown sharply into relief by Rakosi's history of publication between 1923 and 1941 as it may appear to be, his career might seem damaged and his art vulnerable. But to do so is to give implicit assent to a modernist myth of the poet of the sort promulgated, for example, in Pound's repeated interventions on behalf of writers he thought needed rescuing from financial exigency. This is to insert the relations of aristocratic patronage within the quite different social ethos of the artist as professional in a way which ignores the real social relations of the poet in the age of popular media (which began longer ago than we often think) and thus ignores the actual creative matrix of modern poetry. Equally it ignores the fact that a writing block or inhibition is part of the phenomenology of writing. The point in relation to Rakosi is that his stallings, hesitations, and diversions, even his bitter complaints about his situation as a writer, belonged fully to his writing, and contributed to it beyond any call for alle-

Carl Rakosi and Andrew Crozier, Cambridge 1997

viation. It is idle to bewail the notion that a poet has not produced more when he has already written much. If one were tempted to deprecate any aspect of his career it should be borne in mind that Rakosi never committed the authentic sin against poetry of the contemporary poet, forswearing it in the name of a more adult or a more fully social self.

'The Heifer' was dedicated to Jean Crozier and first published as part of Tom Raworth's 'Infolio' series in August 1986.

-o0o-

The Heifer
after Carl Rakosi

From the river bank she saw the fields
with ditches round them full of water.

'The mist had gone. Where were we?'

Striped woollen dress
all morning made our order breakfast
still hungry for more toast and coffee.
The tea-urns bubbled in a corner.

We were together on stools and benches,
at snack-bar counters near the window,
in bars soon after they were open.

'Tell me. Where were we?'

We were inside
both our pasts
and our future
where our paths crossed
                    in a crowded hallway
and the gas-fire of a furnished room
and an early fenland autumn
                    are our memory,

where the light hardened
                    into a shape
and in all directions
                    earth and sky met.

We were where we have not lost
each other's separate power
as if at once
to see together…
the simple tenderness
of a heifer licking a post,
forever lost…
                    forever to be lost.

-o0o-

Crozier's continued interest in the developing work of Carl Rakosi led him to contribute an introduction to the Etruscan Books publication of Rakosi's work The Earth Suite *in 1997:*

> For three-quarters of a century Carl Rakosi has been one of the poets to reckon with; despite legendary years of silence, when his identity became a matter of sometimes bold conjecture, what the work counted for was not forgotten. Among other things, it has registered his experience as both personal – given as his and yet constitutive of what he is – and, into the bargain, exemplary of what it is to be an American. In its composition *The Earth Suite*,

by reconfiguring some later poems with others altogether new, glosses this aspect of his work by methodic emphasis. The great singularities of national identity and destiny fall under the sceptical glance of the twentieth-century democrat who stands witness that representative men are not types of men but symbols of a power that takes itself to be superhuman.

Not 'e pluribus unum' then. En masse the human does not acquire a single face, its voice speaks through its masks: individual types rub along together, not perfectly in harmony, but with degrees of identity. Scrutinised for one emergent apparition, detail under magnification of the exception, the crowd's voices remain a murmur to deaf ears. Rakosi catches in public utterances of private thoughts whatever brings to vivid life the arcana of a common speech as capable of truth as falsehood or ventriloquising the power that would bespeak it. Americana are transcribed up-to-date with an intact folk-wisdom which is as much back-sliding as sure-footed in current circumstance: now, short-lived, tested to self-destruction; now, less fitful, enduring differently, not impatient of recollection. While symbols persist unintelligibly like ontological proofs for dummies to brain themselves on, metaphysics takes a guess at what's under one's nose.

Earthly life may be mortal, but in what once was called the American century it is realised that the living forms we know (Rakosi has been interested in some literally microscopic) are local to our planet, third along from the sun. Now as the century draws to its end we may number its decades with those of Rakosi's life, but he made his come-back too long ago to worry about sounding like an historical personage and besides, his dissidence, although in an honourable tradition, because it is unfamiliar and un-American is too unexpected to sound like an echo, even of himself. To be equally surprised to find recapitulated, in the order of things here, the history of so many lives, a primer for the next century, is surely what follows.

Crozier's interest in the Objectivists was by no means limited to the work of Rakosi. In 1984 he contributed an article on the early poetry of George Oppen to a collection of pieces on modern American poetry edited by R.W. (Herbie) Butterfield in the Critical Studies series published by Vision Press. Continuing this interest, in 1999 he published an essay on Louis Zukofsky in The Objectivist Nexus: Essays in Cultural Poetics, *edited by Rachel Blau DuPlessis and Peter Quartermain.*

-o0o-

Inaugural and Valedictory: The Early Poetry of George Oppen

Although *Of Being Numerous* (1968) and *Primitive* (1978) are arguably George Oppen's mature achievement, rightly attended to and admired as such by many of his readers, these later works are rooted in and a fulfilment of his early work, which they comment on and acknowledge. Yet reference to Oppen's 'early work' incurs immediate uncertainty, since his career can be seen to possess two separate points of departure, first with the poems written in the late '20s and early '30s assembled in *Discrete Series* (1934), and again in the poems of the late '50s and early '60s collected in *The Materials* (1962). To what extent these different beginnings, and the issues raised by the suspension of Oppen's poetic career, either derive from or affect the character of his writing are questions that ask to be explored. To assert peremptorily, with Hugh Kenner, that 'In brief, it took twenty-five years to write the next poem' (although Oppen quotes this remark with approval and apparent relief) is to pre-empt several important questions. To what extent is an Objectivist poetics carried over from *Discrete Series* into *The Materials*? If Oppen did not simply start again where he left off, to what extent is the poetics of *The Materials* responsive to his experience, in the intervening years, of political activism, skilled factory work, infantry combat, family life in post-war America, and political exile in Mexico? Kenner's impatient formula shrinks the issues to fit the case that the contours of Oppen's poetic career can be traced through an as-if uninterrupted series of poems, distorts the relationship between his life and his work and, above all, circumvents consideration of Oppen's politics.

In this essay I propose an account of *Discrete Series* that leads me to conclude that its connection with Oppen's subsequent writing is autobiographical. One way of formulating the difference of *Discrete Series* and *The Materials*, among others, is to point out that whereas in the former there is a recurrent focus on a woman as companion and sexual partner, and on women in general, the latter is pervasively informed by the presence of a child or daughter. Around this figure cluster new issues of age, memory, cultural transmission and temporal process, which both extend and subordinate preoccupations in *Discrete Series* with machinery, work, idleness, and the diverse present-day life of the modern city, all disposed in such a way that time implodes, so to speak, within the simultaneities of the present moment. Oppen's renewed poetic scrutiny of the world, after a prolonged lay-off, produced a more fluent, less cerebral account of what there is, in which value identifies itself more confidently in the things named than it did in the naming of things. As a corollary of this but, I would maintain, preconditionally, *Discrete Series* and *The Materials* confront us with different rhetorics. This in itself might be taken as evidence of a fundamental discontinuity in Oppen's work. It is in terms of these rhetorics, totalities of the formal and discursive procedures of the writing, that any reading of Oppen, especially, must answer for itself, so much otherwise does his work seem incommensurate with writing with which we stand on more familiar terms. By and large existing discussions of *Discrete Series* have tended to describe its formal qualities as embodiments of some of the given features of modern poetic style, and given little attention to any specific discursive assumptions they might be bound up with. The Objectivist notion of a poem as a made thing, as a machine, has tended to confer on the reductive, almost (it might seem) arbitrary writing of *Discrete Series* a craftsmanlike authority and prestige that have gone largely unargued. The language strategies and decisions implicit in the writing, of which it is the outcome, have been readily taken for granted, neither analysed nor justified in relation to the interpretations they enable or forestall.

Discrete Series was an almost belated event within a briefly coherent literary milieu, the imprint of which it bore clearly but ambiguously. Oppen was associated with a grouping of young poets, convened initially in the pages of Ezra Pound's *Exile* (1927–28), where work by Carl Rakosi and Louis Zukofsky appeared, at a moment when Pound was anxious to consolidate and put on record the achievement of the previous fifteen years, and was looking for American disciples into the bargain. Rakosi and Zukofsky were put in touch with each other, and also with William Carlos Williams and other native survivors of Pound's generation. Pound wished this small force of younger poets to manifest itself as the new generation, and arranged for Zukofsky to edit the February 1931 issue of *Poetry* for this purpose. *An 'Objectivists' Anthology* (1932), edited by Zukofsky and published by Oppen, established more explicitly, though with less publicity, the short-lived connection of the new generation and their predecessors. There are grounds for seeing Pound's *Active Anthology* (1933), which included Zukofsky and Oppen, though not Rakosi, as a late manifestation of Objectivism, although Pound's waning interest can be inferred from his comment that many of the young poets seem to have 'lost contact with language as language… in particular Mr Zukofsky's Objectivists seem prone to this error'. Nevertheless, when *Discrete Series* came out the following year it carried a Preface by Pound saluting 'a serious craftsman, a sensibility which…has not been got out of any other man's books'.

Oppen was by no means a prominent member of this milieu. He sponsored To Publishers, later The Objectivist Press, and saw to the production side of things. Apart from *An 'Objectivists' Anthology* the enterprise is best known for having published books by Williams and Pound. Oppen published very little of his own work: two poems in the February 1931 issue of *Poetry* that Zukofsky edited, and another four in January 1932; one poem in *An 'Objectivists' Anthology*; five in *Active Anthology*. Eight of the twelve were included in *Discrete Series*. His junior status was seized upon in reviews of his book. Not much good came to him either of Pound's Preface or an enthusiastic review by Williams in the July 1934 issue of *Poetry*; if anything, such connections defined Oppen too narrowly, and comparisons were made at his expense by, for example, Geoffrey Grigson and H.R. Hays. Grigson objected to 'simple brevity' ('a push-bike for the simple-minded'), and found that 'when one attempts to permit these anti-poems to expand in one's mind…one discovers them to be elastic, not organic – fictions which can only be enlarged by pulling.' For Hays, Oppen's 'pretentiousness is not supported by any felicity of observation', and whereas 'Williams is intent on capturing the object as a whole; Oppen is apparently trying to derive textures of objects.'

It could hardly have turned out otherwise, perhaps. What prestige had either Pound or Williams to confer at a time when they still published with such hole-and-corner operations as The Objectivist Press? As much as anything, they were convenient sticks with which to beat poets who attended to their outworn example. And *Discrete Series* cannot have seemed an ingratiating or rewarding book. it is tightly organised, even rigid, and gives very little away. It consists of thirty-one short poems, the first of which, with its pastiche of a Jamesian periodic sentence, is sufficiently anomalous in style to ask to be regarded as standing outside an even more tightly-knit group of thirty poems. The sense that this poem is in some way prefatory is reinforced both by its promulgation of large-scale thematic concerns in its concluding reference to 'the world, weather swept, with which one shares the century' and by its implicit repudiation of the values and conventions of Oppen's wealthy middle-class background and also, I would argue, their attendant boredom. The narrow line trodden here between boredom as knowledge of the world and boredom as a particular knowledge of the world is typical of the close shave Oppen's way with definitions and propositions administers. Neither the book's programme nor the terms in which it is proposed can put us at our ease. The book appears, if anything, almost too deliberately calculated, with an unconcealed but obscure polemic intention; it is decidedly self-possessed, and comments on its properties as it proceeds, as something both written and read, in a way that seems to attribute both graphic and three-dimensional qualities to its existence. It is so little like the majority of young poets' 'first books', neither haphazard miscellany nor an object of subsequent shame, that it might almost be taken for a valedictory rather than an inaugural statement. Indeed, it already bears traces of the diagnosis of social disaster that led Oppen to quietly abandon poetry (including the option of politically committed poetry) and take up the life of a full-time Communist Party worker in Brooklyn and subsequently in Utica.

The very title of *Discrete Series* is a sign of deliberate intent. Series are normally continuous, each term in succession deriving from its predecessors and determining those that follow. Oppen's later elucidation of his intended meaning represents it in terms that do not appear to have occurred to his readers at the time. Grigson thought that the writing itself was discrete, and gave credit at least for the fact that it had 'no pinned-on imagery'. Williams, on the other hand, thought that the term was probably 'meant merely to designate a series separate from other series'. Oppen's account of what he had in view, however, might well put us in mind of the position taken by Samuel Johnson in his 'Review of a Free Enquiry' (1757), namely that our partial knowledge of the creation, unbuttressed by theories of plenitude, is not inconsistent with feelings of awe in the face of a transcendent origin of being. Oppen describes a discrete series as 'a series of terms each of which is empirically derived, each of which is empirically true'. This empiricism was to be made to yield a method, in an 'attempt to construct meaning, to construct a method of thought from the imagist technique of poetry – from the imagist intensity of vision', based on 'a moment, an actual time, when you believe something to be true, and you construct a meaning from these moments of conviction.' Elsewhere Oppen has remarked that the numbers 14, 28, 38, 42 comprise an exemplary discrete series: 'the names of the stations on the east side subway'. Yet the intelligibility of such a series depends on a context of independent knowledge, some actual or theoretical reference. If after catching the Tube at Victoria I find myself at Earl's Court, I know that I am on the District Line, not the Circle , and that I am on the wrong train for Kensington High Street.

Oppen's comments, thirty or more years in retrospect, need to be approached with due caution. The appeal to conviction, for example, seems more fully in keeping with his concerns of the 1960s. The evidence of the few poems Oppen published prior to *Discrete Series* is helpful in this respect. It is clear both that he initially thought of some of the poems in *Discrete Series* under a different rubric, and that 'discrete series' was a generic term rather than a title designating a specific text. The two poems he published in the February 1931 issue of *Poetry* were jointly titled '1930'S', as was his poem in *An 'Objectivists' Anthology*. These three poems, arranged in a different order, became the first three poems of *Discrete Series*: the prefatory poem, and a pair numbered 1 and 2 to denote their correlation. This pair of poems refers to skyscraper lobbies and lunch-bars, and on the basis of this rendering of the texture of contemporary life, and the topical connotations of the discarded title, it might be concluded that for a time Oppen contemplated a series of poems in a contemporary documentary vein, but subsequently revised this intention to produce a more rigorous conception of the composition of a serial work. The term 'Discrete Series' first appeared as the collective title for Oppen's group of four poems in the January 1932 issue of *Poetry*, but of this group only one – the last – is to be found in *Discrete Series*. The first three poems refer to the confined orbit of the poet's room, the inadequacy to passionate life of the world of social refinement, and anticipations of the release of summer. They provide an antithetical version of city life, in which wished-for dialogue keeps giving way to fretful monologue. 'Cat-Boat', the concluding poem, is different; it objectifies the tense intersections of mast, sail, wind, water and sun as a single event, and now the beleaguered couple implied in the previous poems can glide unscathed over the infinite peril of the 'unrimmed holes' of the sea-bed. If in this series there is a sequence from alienation to fulfilment, its preliminaries contribute little to the outcome; their rôle within the discursive framework is at best thematic. The complex stasis of 'Cat-Boat' (for in fact the perils glide 'beneath us') is not subject to the recognition of directed feeling tone, but is the source of its own security. Even though the terms of this series are arguably discrete, in the sense that they are not derived successively from each other, there remains a definite sense of forward movement under schematic pressure (both in terms of seasonal progression and spiritual attainment), the initial stages of which, in relation to 'Cat-Boat', are finally redundant. The boat has no need to negotiate terms with its situation since it is so completely borne by and one with it.

Whereas the contradictions encountered in the first three poems are organised propositionally or interrogatively, their discourse articulated by means of an enacted central consciousness, in the final poem the contradiction between security and risk is sited without disrupting the sequence of indicative statements ('imagist statements') by anything more than a break in the line, the graphic/prosodic device indicating a shift in the weight the poem is carrying. The transition of feeling and evaluation between one reference and another has not been attributed to an imputed subject, and the poem's significance is thereby normative, in the absence of such personal witness, if the reader agrees. It is possible to imagine a series of such poems, imposing their conviction of the way things are or might be on their own evidence. But any such gain is accompanied by considerable risk, for the reader of *Discrete Series* is aware, as much as anything, of language operating under severe pressure, of a discourse loaded and compressed in order to test individual words. Far from being a dance of the intellect among words, Oppen's logopoeia implies considerable scepticism about available discourses and communal usage.

I allude to Pound's category deliberately, because Oppen's references to imagism, in particular his suggestion that it might provide a mode of thought, point beyond general notions of imagism as a technique of immediate presentation. In his Preface to *Discrete Series* Pound endeavoured to distinguish between Oppen's work and that of Williams, but this is misleading. Pound himself, if anyone, is the presiding influence in *Discrete Series*, even though Oppen's field of reference may remind us more of Williams than of Pound, and this influence is most discernible when we trace the basic strategies of Oppen's writing. At the same time, Pound's influence does not result in any very clear resemblance, for Oppen adopts Pound's method only to throw it into reverse. In Pound's typically imagist poems we find a discourse constructed through the juxtaposition of elements, normally drawn from different conceptual orders of reality, the spiritual and the mundane. These elements are not so much opposed or contrasted as shown in terms of their possible equivalence, the completion of this discourse lying in some further, unstated term. The advantage of this method for Pound, which we might epitomise as the reciprocity of image and ideogram, is that elements so used, by virtue of their difference, can be scaled up or down, either by setting them parallel to other series of elements, or by subdivision into new series. The disadvantage of this method is the monolithic unity of concept it entails; its inclusivity breaks down under the weight of its own inertia – as we find in the *Cantos* – when it is developed beyond certain limits. This is experienced either as incoherence or as vulnerability to counter-discourses.

The poems in *Discrete Series* have a binary structure similar to that of the Poundian image, but whereas in Pound the elements correlated are different but equivalent, in Oppen they are similar (ontologically identical in some cases) but opposed. It is out of the collision of different versions of similar events, the discovery of mendacity or misrepresentation where discourses compete, that the meanings of *Discrete Series* arise. One of the book's least startling poems can exemplify Oppen's general procedure.

The edge of the ocean,
The shore: here
Somebody's lawn,
By the water.

On the face of it this is a charming vignette, suggestive perhaps of nature tamed to serve as an amenity to civilised living. But to read the poem thus is an act of selective attention, hardly adequate to the already stripped-down syntax. In the absence of explicit grammatical co-ordinators (there is no main verb, for example, and the consequent power vacuum destabilises the adverb 'here') our reading is forced to rely more than usual on the interaction of semantic values, and indeed the poem immediately indicates that it is concerned with definitions. Surely in such extreme verbal economy there is no space for any surplus. If we give each word its due weight, we see that the poem turns on the opposition of 'shore' and 'lawn', 'ocean' and 'water', names for the same things in this instance, for we still understand a reference outside the terms of the poem to some actual situation, of which the poem's two opposed discourses are minimal predications. We are not even permitted the interval of relief that might be afforded by a here/there contrast: the 'here' of immediate location is shunted forward (a colon marks the point of impact) from a preliminary definition, if not to repossess 'somebody's lawn' at least to show how private property diminished the natural world. 'Here' man's triumph over nature has been achieved at the public expense, if 'shore' and 'ocean' are the proper names for those things as they locate and define the conditions of human existence. But in the world this poem refers to the elemental conditions of our existence, on the edge of which we live, are seen to be hidden. They are obscured by such an innocent, domesticated little word as 'lawn', which under testing pressure reveals the weight of ethical censure. We can hardly feel, however, that the judgement here proceeds from concern for popular rights, from some sense of exclusion; the perceptions deployed in this poem are derived from somewhere beyond the social, beyond the edge of the inhabitable world and human history. If we want to look for this place, we should refer to the conclusion of Oppen's prefatory poem. If 'By the water' could stand for 'The edge of the ocean', the measure of the earth's waters would be taken on a scale that found them no bigger than a duck pond.

With this exemplary poem in mind, and seeing it in the light of Oppen's dismemberment of the original 'Discrete Series', it becomes possible to generalise the assumptions and procedures directing the writing of *Discrete Series*. In the first place, the poems are written in a way that does not permit them to be read progressively, as though leading the reader forward to some conclusion to be enacted at the moment of textual closure. (This can be understood to apply to the series as a whole.) The reader is required to bear in mind concurrently all the elements in a particular poem. But if the poems are non-narrative, no more are they the random and simultaneous notations of a moment; their detail is neither additive, accumulative, nor typical. Detail is organised to establish lines of association and dissociation, the parameters of discourses local to the poem. Moreover, language itself is treated as an empirical datum, in which reference is inextricably combined with its terminology; language cannot, on such assumptions, mediate neutrally between the reader and some other matrix of empirical knowledge. (Oppen's work contains no gestures towards authenticity of speech such as we find in Williams, for example.) Hence verbs cannot be relied upon to correlate relationships between details, so that throughout *Discrete Series* we find that transitive functions are regularly displaced onto adverbs and prepositions, and that participles and intransitive verbs are favoured.

In the light of the implications of Oppen's methods Hays's strictures on *Discrete Series* are seen to have at least some descriptive accuracy, for one important outcome of Oppen's procedure, we might say its very purpose, is a general levelling of usual figure/ground gradients. Oppen can take objects very much for granted, both as cultural and perceptual products. Motor cars and yachts, whatever their different values, are empirically very simple. Similarly, Oppen has little time for the braveries of figurative rhetoric. Both types of figure/ground relationship, the perceptual *gestalt* and the rhetorical trope, divert attention from the system or ground in which the figure is produced. In poetry that addresses the reader in terms of an array of figures it is always possible to see how the figures are produced within the general terms of the discourse, but it is not really feasible to provide them also with the empirical substantiation we find in *Discrete Series*. This is a mainly negative observation, as regards Oppen, and need not stop anyone from thinking of the poems in *Discrete Series* as discrete tropes if it is thought useful to do so. The substantive issue, in Oppen's practice, has to do with the way our knowledge of productive systems or grounds tends to be abstract and theoretical, subordinate to the configurations and entities they give rise to. 'Texture' is an approximate but less than adequate term by which to denote the outcome of Oppen's over-riding interest in retrieving the commonplace background of everyday life – pavements and street-lighting, systems of communication and transfer – in an attempt to bring within the range of discourse conditions normally taken for granted or imperceptible. (It is in terms of such a project, entailing the textual absence of determinate entities, that Zukofsky's remark that Oppen's work deals with the 'void' makes best sense.) By taking basal conditions as the contexts for discursive juxtapositions in *Discrete Series*, Oppen is able in effect to figure one theoretical order of reality and its discourse against the ground of another.

Resistance of the solicitation of trope and *gestalt* leads to different kinds of engagement, but in each different case we can see that the outcome is compatible with the need to produce a textual effect of continuous groundwork. The fifth poem of *Discrete Series*, for example, starts with a series of attributive figures similar to those deployed by Williams at the beginning of 'Portrait of a Lady'.

Her ankles are watches
(Her arm-pits are causeways for water)...

But these appropriative figures are checked and replaced by a more literal incursive discourse as the woman in question continues her morning routine ('She walks on a sphere//Walks on the carpet) so that her everyday, insignificant gestures reappropriate her being.

Her movement accustomed, abstracted,
Declares this morning a woman's
'My hair, scalp – '.

Here a continuous ground, between woman and morning, is established thematically and, to an extent, figuratively. The seventh poem, in contrast, specifies and comments on a setting for events that remain elusive.

The lights, paving –
This important device
Of a race

Remains till morning.

Burns
Against the wall.
He has chosen a place
With the usual considerations,
Without stating them.
Buildings.

Is this poem about the streets or the city authorities? What sort of race is referred to: the human race, or an athletic contest? Who is the referent of the abruptly intrusive pronoun? The poem provides no answers to such questions. What it does is dissociate the terms normally subsumed in such concepts as 'city' or 'environment' in order to divest such fictions of their contingency. However depopulated this urban night-scene appears, it is hardly mysterious; nor is it void of human purpose, however disavowed its social ideologies may be. The two discourses opposed in this poem interrupt one another, so that the reader is left in the dark about the precise character of each, but as they intersect their separate details combine in a different discourse, however fragmentary, which produces the base conditions of social forms and agencies. The transition from 'wall' to 'place', between location and decision, mediates the two discourses while indicating their discrepancy; the referent for 'he' can then be found, if anywhere, in 'a race'.

Throughout *Discrete Series* objects and configurations tend to be merged with temporal and spatial sequences, either by repetition or dispersal. In the eighteenth poem a bird – probably one of Williams's sparrows – is epistemologically complex within the terms of recurrent experience. In the twenty-sixth poem the Depression spectacle of a man selling postcards in the street is part and parcel of the urban scenery of traffic and cinema publicity. We might say that within the terms of Oppen's method the presentation of a determinate figure would be seen as a failure, since such an achievement would entail the subordination of one discourse to another by a too explicit inflection of the ground that the poems equally derive from and have as their formal aim. Oppen's suppression of significant figuration is perhaps most blatant, in terms of the available discourses of the '30s, when the poems raise the issue of photography. Here we can gauge both the extent to which Oppen distanced himself from any documentary intention, and the degree of his difference from Williams. The 'readers' of documentary photographs are presented, in familiar language, with information that is remote from their experience. Their empirical relationship with such images is not corroborative but guaranteed by notions of authenticity, although the assumed values of authenticity are effectively subordinate to confrontation. The last people a documentary image is for are the people depicted in it. But where photographs are most clearly acknowledged as Oppen's sources in *Discrete Series*, they are treated as snapshots, their subject matter grounded in familiarity. In the seventeenth poem, for instance, which refers to what is presumably one of Brady's civil war photographs, we find 'The cannon of that day/In our parks'. In several other poems the reader can infer that reference is made to a photographic image.

> This land:
> The hills, round under straw;
> A house
>
> With rigid trees
>
> And flaunts
> A family laundry,
> And the glass of windows

This reminds us, more than anything else, surely, of that 1930s photography of American landscape dominated by commercial signs, and we can see inscribed among the details of the poem a Walker Evans image of a window bearing the legend 'Family Laundry' somewhere in the middle of nowhere. If I am right to see this (and I could extend such speculations to deal with other instances, the tenth poem for example), it is because Oppen appeals to the inclusiveness of the photographic image, its inability to state preferences within its visual field. In this respect Oppen stands in marked contrast to Williams who, as Bram Dijkstra has shown, used Stieglitz's photographs to explore significant configurations of resistance between one object and another within the strict margins of the image.

In his Preface to *An 'Objectivists' Anthology* Zukofsky designated 'condensation' as the technique by which the necessary craftsmanship of contemporary verse was hidden in the poem-object. 'Against obvious transitions, Pound, Williams, Rakosi, Bunting, Miss Moore oppose condensation. The transitions cut are implicit in the work, 3 or 4 things occur at a time making the difference between Aristotelian expansive unities and the concentrated locus which is the mind acting creatively upon the facts.' Zukofsky's polemic opposition of particulars to generalisation was not espoused by Oppen, but if we put Oppen within this general stylistic context, we might more precisely define his technique by saying that, while in his work the notion of the mind operating directly among facts remained problematic precisely because it showed the mediated nature of facts, he does indeed use condensation in order to effect transitions. We might go further and say that we recognise that a transition occurs while remaining in ignorance of the facts. The separate poems of *Discrete Series* are related by method as well as technique, but above all they are related by their collective reference to a presence of a continuum outside their series – the inferred continuum of the world accessible to empirical knowledge, however full of gaps that world might be. This reference occurs within the qualified and incomplete discourses the poems set in motion, and it is as an accompaniment of the friction generated by the inadequacy of specific discourses that a conviction of a totality beyond them arises. But there are neither large-scale axioms to provide a framework for an inclusive knowledge, nor the full discourse of a continuously knowing subject. We feel the presence of consistent intelligence in the poems' method, of a certain sensibility in the range of empirical details responded to and acknowledged, but this intelligence and sensibility are not projected within the series as a point of view from which its various components are rendered intelligible as a whole. That is up to the reader. Above all, the reader is forced to resist any temptation to search for and identify with an authorial point of view, for the author can only occasionally be made out as another presence among the empirical data (a 'me' rather than an 'I') or heard as one voice amongst others.

When Oppen began to write again in 1958, shortly before his return to the U.S.A. from his Mexican exile, he did, in one sense, start again where he left off in 1934, for the poems in *The Materials* deal centrally with the relationship between the human, individual and social, and the non-human world. But Oppen's procedures had to be radically different, inasmuch as starting from this point he effectively claimed authorship of the meanings of his earlier work along with the experience and memory of the intervening years. *The Materials* is extensively organised, in a way that *Discrete Series* is not, through coordinated thematic centres, and authenticates itself by referring back to a reflective consciousness, however scrupulous and hesitant its voice may be in stating and weighing the internal resistances of its meanings. But what was perhaps crucial in enabling this different beginning was Oppen's recognition of the divergence of the chronologies of the individual organism and the world it lives in, sharpened by the knowledge that under thermo-nuclear threat those chronologies might for once converge and close.

VII
ON BRITISH POETRY

The following essay on Roy Fisher began as a commission for a Donald Davie festschrift on his retirement from Vanderbilt, but was rejected on the grounds that not enough had yet been written about Fisher. Crozier extended the piece to develop the connections between 'Introit' and City *before publishing it in* PN Review, *Volume 18, Number 3, January/February 1992. In a letter to me of 21 October 2004 Crozier commented on Fisher's reaction to what Davie had written about him in his 1973 appraisal of the effect of Thomas Hardy on contemporary British poetry: 'When* Thomas Hardy and British Poetry *was published I remember that Fisher was dismayed – no, seriously upset and offended – by what Davie said about him. If what he had said about his own writing can be taken seriously then of course he was right to be.'*

-o0o-

Signs of Identity: Roy Fisher's A Furnace

1

Roy Fisher commented with some asperity on Donald Davie's 'Appreciation' of him in *Thomas Hardy and British Poetry* – 'I wasn't aware that he'd exactly written about *my* work in that book!' – yet the chapter on Fisher is generous in its willingness to admire writing Davie does not, it is apparent, find immediately congenial. Davie points to Fisher's descriptive power, his technical scruple, and the kind of verse in which he is most skilful and distinguished. He draws attention to an opacity in Fisher's language produced by the weight attached to particular words, 'conscience' for example, by repeated use. In what concerns the manner and procedure of Fisher's writing, and its engagement with the reader, Davie's observations remain the best introduction to Fisher's work, even though the detail and tendency of his argument provoke exasperated disagreement. Davie is surely mistaken, for instance, in the claim that in Larkin's 'Afternoons' and Fisher's 'As He Came Near Death' there are lines in which 'the act of the imagination is identical'. He is also tendentious, for the point is made in anticipation of the argument by which

Fisher is seen to typify the condition of the modern British literary imagination: he opts for the social rather than the human, for pathos rather than tragedy. These categories and the argument they serve do indeed say more about Davie, and his rueful acceptance of the condition thus diagnosed, than they say about Fisher.

Fisher's recent long poem *A Furnace* connects explicitly with the earlier work discussed by Davie, so that his 'Appreciation' is more than ever helpful by virtue of the very disagreements it occasions. For Davie both Fisher and Larkin are poets of cultural compromise and adjustment, the modernist credentials sported by Fisher mere flourishes, deplorable but incidental. The compromise Davie has in mind represents the terms on which high culture must adjust to the democracy of the common man. This may be true of Larkin, but for Fisher, surely, the terms of adjustment would need to be reversed; he is, on the contrary, less well adjusted than Davie would like to think, and no upholder of those myths about popular power and agency in which the image of society is illuminated only by pathos. What differentiates Larkin and Fisher goes beyond matters of formal device, as Davie suggests, Fisher's 'making strange' as against Larkin's 'choice epithet and strategically reversed foot'. In Larkin's phrase 'pushing them to the side of their own lives' the reflexive force of 'their own' produces the affective space in which such displacement can be seen to occur. The pathos is subtle; colloquialism modifies the more conventionally troped pathos of 'Their beauty has thickened'. Indeed, sealed in their reflexivity the young mothers of 'Afternoons' wear pathos as a mark of identity and reconciliation. The imagination is here subordinate to the topic of mutability, specifically the brevity of female beauty, and acts dramatically by providing a figurative scenario of insensitive jostling and shoving. Fisher's phrase 'worked out on to the skin of his life', although its syntax is simpler, is more complex than Larkin's in its imaginative act. There is no discontinuity within what is predicated of the subject, no interval for figurative play against literal intention, as adverb and preposition bind the verb into the space in which it acts. There is, however, some risk of excess specification. Why not, for example, 'his skin' rather than 'the skin of his life'? There is little colloquial resonance to be had from 'skin of his', or 'worked out' for that matter, for Fisher's diction observes the common denotations of its separate words. Nevertheless, the number of meanings of 'work' that might contribute to our sense of what is going on is potentially excessive: to resolve, to disengage, to cover a surface. The act of the imagination here is bound up with notions of extension, recumbency, and suspension, that are felt to be opposed to an undeclarable and fugitive sense of identity and being. What is imagined is not a change of personal fortune but a transformation involving loss of physical presence, the identity of the dying man shown in the process of turning into an inscription – the bare memory of him – on the bodiless surface to which his life is being reduced. The alienation is radical, without redemptive possibility, and excludes pathos. The act of the imagination in language is equally radical, for what is figured in language, the working out and the skin of life, is also propositional. Larkin's 'of their own lives', with its apparently guileless emphasis, uses reflexivity as a device to internalise the figure of pushing aside and mitigate his characteristic theme of the hatred between generations by subordinating it to one of humanism's major topics. Fisher's 'of his life' completes the working out, for the time being, of complex responses to the experience of identity and death.

Larkin and Fisher share a certain field of empirical observation, and Davie can justly say that when reading them we may exclaim 'this is how it is!' But Larkin's observation is set off against the massive stability of a cultural tradition, and if Fisher does not harness observation by similar means he is not thereby disablingly immersed in it. He may seem esoteric in his search for meanings, but his findings are kept provisional. It is tendentious to chide Fisher for not making clear statements or issuing definitive judgements, and what Davie attributes to technical deficiency would more properly be seen as marking the excessive character of the common language to which Fisher scrupulously restricts himself. It is by their alignment to a cultural tradition to which Fisher has owned no allegiance that such binary oppositions as pathos and tragedy, the social and the human, acquire meaning. When Davie identifies Fisher's position as anti-Lawrencian in its denial of 'the intensities and ecstasies of the sexual and personal life' he defers to that tradition, setting Lawrence against Hardy, the sexual with the personal and human against the social, and is prevented from recognising that in Fisher sexual intimacy and ecstasy belong equally with the social fabric of ordinary life.

2

Davie's verdict that Fisher remained 'most challengingly the author of *City*' was entirely just, but if my objections to Davie's categories are well founded – and it is in *City* that Davie detects Fisher settling for the social as opposed to the human – then he is wrong to say that it is 'a work of sustained pathos...constructed carefully in that mode around a centre...in which the pathos is at its most intense'. I can agree that 'Starting to Make a Tree' has a particular salience, and almost agree that it is 'grotesque and touching', but it does not touch me with *pity*. Indeed, ramshackle and ill-equipped as they are, the *ad hoc* cosmographers of this section of the poem are only to be pitied from the standpoint of an imperial and confident tradition which, it is Fisher's point, the city has always lacked. The absence of such a tradition is signified by the inscription of the common noun as the poem's proper name, as it is by the poem's textual perplexities, which the poet reinscribes in his own person as the poem's eye witness. The sustaining mode of *City* is not pathos but alienation, the alienation of the observer from his world, of that world from its past, of life from death, and Fisher's 'making strange' is the very sign of that alienation. The observer's own life, the past of the city, sexuality and death, are thrown into question, conditions of existence that struggle for expression against the grain of their locale, but which obtain recognition there by Fisher's observation of their negation or occlusion in the presence of the city's corporate signs. Or so I take Fisher to mean when he writes of the city that 'Most of it has never been seen'.

A Furnace is the counterpart of *City* in scale and ambition, prefigured by it and its revision. But whereas the unity of the formal construction of *City*, a loose assemblage of pieces of prose and verse, can only be ascertained retrospectively, in *A Furnace* the parts bear a figural correspondence to the whole. A sequence of seven movements opens from an 'Introit', similar to them in construction, but held to a single passage of reference and reflection. A Preface offers hints rather than exegesis. When Fisher says, for example, '*A Furnace* is a poem containing a certain amount of history', he might seem to place it within the Poundian tradition of epic. But if its scope may be taken to be epic it might equally appear to be written in the prophetic mode. The reader, proceeding beyond the 'Introit' to immediately encounter reference to 'the pit', might suppose the allusion to be anatomical, but might equally, and more plausibly associate the pit with the poem's title and be reminded of the Biblical apocalypse: 'and there arose a smoke out of the pit, as the smoke of a great furnace' (*Revelations* IX, 2). But this will not quite do, and not merely in the absence of the scatological frenzy such imagery can evoke. Furnaces smoke in the poem ('the bloomery/used to smoke up in the woods/under the green chapel'), but not enough to smother us in apocalyptic intimations, and the Preface also remarks of the poem that 'its fire is Heraclitean, and will not give off much Gothic smoke'. It is not, then, a poem exclusively about last things: 'Apocalypse/lies within time, as these beings/may or may not so lie: if they do,/their demeanour could equally match/the beginning of all things.' Endings and beginnings together are more aptly Heraclitean and, since Heraclitean fire is both the principle of change in all things and the universe itself (*Fragments* 28, 29, Wheelwright translation), it might then seem that *A Furnace* has the cosmos figured into its proper name. But *A Furnace*, the Preface states first of all, is also a device to 'assist natural processes of change; to persuade obstinate substances to alter', and 'some of the substances fed in are very solid indeed'. The reader must expect references that are resistant and heavy with the specifics of history and locale, but also far-flung in time and space, from the raising of the Grand Fleet at Scapa Flow to the dismantling of Consett steel-works, from the last British tour of Coleman Hawkins to the successive site plans of Trier, from the watershed of the Staffordshire moorlands to the formation of clouds. It might be helpful also to recall that in Heraclitus another of fire's properties is that it 'throws apart and then brings together again' (Fragment 31).

Annotation of *A Furnace* is not called for, however, because reference in Fisher is not to a body of knowledge from which the poetic acquires power. Indeed, the process whereby Fisher's solid substances 'show relativities which would otherwise remain hidden in their concreteness' suggests the reverse. Nevertheless, if Fisher's information is miscellaneous its use is exemplary rather than casual, and the point has some bearing on Davie's disparagement of 'mere enumeration' when he compares the devices used by Fisher and Larkin. Davie's judgements are backed by a linkage of knowledge and authority which is occulted by critical approval of the effects it produces of deft economy of utterance, but it is to knowledge and authority as separate issues that our attention is drawn by Fisher's deployment of the figure of the charlatan, who must seek understanding without guidance or instruction.

> Sudden and grotesque
> callings. Grown man
> without right learning; by nobody
> guided to the places; not knowing
> what might speak; having eased awkwardly
> into the way of being called.

Such self-reference is sparse but crucial to the poem's acts of imaginative self-definition, its testing of difference and identity, made possible by the *rite de passage* represented by *Wonders of Obligation* and its celebration of the multiplicity of the particular. Fisher's comment is stiff, without self-pity or illusion. If its negations do not expose traditionless making-do as incapacitating, no more do they admit the converse of tradition, the private oracular revelation, except as an irruptive and incomprehensible attraction that breaks through in certain places as a sign of discrepancy.

Such places exist 'on their own account, not/for anybody's comfort', and are presented through Fisher's characteristic attention to urban surface and mass: 'Iron walls/tarred black, and discoloured,/towering'. Although such places afford 'gigantic peace' the specific 'open space, marked out with/ tramlines in great curves among blue/Rowley Rag paving bricks' is 'Forbidden', 'Not a place for stopping and spying.' Here as elsewhere in *A Furnace* the alienated mode of the *City* observer is called into question by the reach of feeling that is discovered in the colossal and abandoned remnants of a derelict industrial culture. Fisher is not another Volney, however; ruin and revolution occur together on a scale either too short ('I have seen such things worked rapidly,/in my lifetime') or too long ('A pick-handle or a boot/.../or what was/flung as a stone,/having come slowly on/out of a cloudiness in the sea') to afford them joint leverage on the present. And of course such places are not entirely secret or devoid of function.

> The single human refuge
> a roadside urinal, rectangular
> roofless sarcophagus of tile and brick,
> topped round with spikes and
> open to the sky.

'Sarcophagus' is more than a conceit on the pomp of old-fashioned civic architecture and the disposal of human waste. Its association with 'refuge' reiterates a main topic of *A Furnace*, the connection of the living to the dead, one's own life and death. The connection is close because the distinction is never permanent: 'that you are dead/.../recedes and recurs often'. And just as much as revelations are incomprehensible the oracular mode in *A Furnace* is ineloquent in its association with death: the dead have 'no news', ancestors have 'certificates but no stories'. 'Birmingham voices in the entryways/lay the law down', but what law is not enunciated, and were it heard the demotic of those voices, as the colloquial phrase suggests, would be powerless and without authority.

Birmingham voice
hollow under the dark
arch of the entryway,

by slow torsion wrenched
out of her empty jaw, sunk
hole of lips; no way it could be
understood or answered.

Here the 'old language' of Birmingham and the 'slow-dying woman' whose sybilline speech it is converge in recollected childhood experience, and the whole cycle within history of the area of industrial housing where Fisher was born and grew up is inscribed, 'year after year from the beginning' – from first being built, through self-respecting fear of neighbours, the child's 'early learning', and the 'primordial life' of an aged first inhabitant whose death is 'modern and nothing, a weekend in the Cold War'. And just as her life was powerful in its resemblance of death, her husband's death is presented as powerful in its resemblance of life. Life and death, Fisher suggests, are most completely sundered by the social agencies of an authority from whose meanings ordinary lives are excluded. And if the 'life of the dead' is hidden, made appalling to contemplate – unlike the 'graves in the sky,/companies of lives lifted up' of prehistoric societies – is it surprising that the oracular mode can operate only as parody? Revelations in *A Furnace*, if they occur, will do so by other means.

3

Throughout *A Furnace* textual correlation attaches incremental significance to particular passages, and underwrites interpretation: the correlation of 'right' and 'early learning'; of the death-in-life of the 'slow-dying woman' and of the decrepit Coleman Hawkins, of his 'mutter and chuckle across the mouthpiece' and 'the image, dues mortuus,/death chuckling along in its life'; of 'Neighbour-fear/for the children' and 'the work-/ing class streets where work and wages/hid, as the most real shame.' The ramifying correlations of the text might probably be plotted from part through counterpart to leave little of the poem unaccounted for. But these correlations are not formally signified; even where what is imagined is bred out of correlation the parts are first of all distinct, and correlate across the reader's recollection or anticipation. To suggest otherwise would be to insist that *A Furnace* is a self-enclosed, hermetic text, whereas its writing is so grounded in specifics of sensibility and attention that the world of empirical reference is constantly interrogated, disclosed not as familiar but other. 'Is that how it is?'

The point has already been made that it is not any intrinsic character of the substances fed into the poem that confers meaning. Substance is allowed to retain its separate identity: Fisher's method is not that of Symbolist correspondence by which substance is spiritualised on to a plane of higher meaning. Meaning depends on correlations established by techniques of recurrence and variation, equivalence and transformation – modes of relation that the writing must first activate if it is to enunciate its meanings. To approach these matters is to approach the characteristic and enabling features of the writing, the contingent and intentional structures of the rhetoric by which meaning is governed. What I have in mind has already been touched on – common speech, textual excess or surplus, amalgamation of propositional and figurative modes – but a fuller outline is required of the procedures on which the intellectual and formal complexity of *A Furnace* is based.

When I mentioned the risk of excessive specification in the line from 'As He Came Near Death' the hazard I had in mind was of being misread. What I now wish to show is that as *surplus* such specification is not just a feature of style in Fisher's writing, not a potential defect but one of the signs by which he is read: an agent of organisation and connection in the text. The term 'surplus' denotes a cluster of practices predisposed by and significant of explicit but equivocal attitudes to language and value, conditioned in their turn by divergent attitudes to meaning: that it is both the predicate of a known objective reality and, at the same time, the outcome of the gathering and reproduction of signs. Theoretical ambivalence of this sort does not, needless to say, necessarily manifest itself in poetry as incoherence or antagonistic self-contradiction.

In the early poem 'Quarry Hills' Fisher observes a new housing development and draws a contrast between 'comfort' and 'desolation', between domesticity and a tract of derelict land on which houses are built. It is a poem of descriptive detail and nuance, attentive to the signs of inhabitation and use, but also on terms of familiarity with the type of scene described. The observed particulars are separately and appropriately qualified: 'cemetery', 'slimed', 'rickety and ageing', 'dwarfish', 'eaten through'. In this list only 'cemetery', used adjectivally to describe the new gardens, is at all startling, but the transferred use commands the assent of recognition. Like the other words its use is justified by its contribution to scrupulous denotation of matters of fact. Yet listed together these words are alarming and ominous; they suggest another discourse, and the presence of feeling which, although not textually suppressed, has not been given a voice. What I draw attention to is not a foregrounded pattern of imagery that directs the reader's current of feeling. Each term fits its descriptive occasion, with almost neutral precision, and acts discretely, not sequenced with others in a crescendo of blight. Yet some or all of them persist as the after-image of what has been observed, a surplus of textual signs detached from the significance each has borne in description. This surplus might be taken as indicative of an affective motive for description, but if so the poem must be thought all the more scrupulous for not signifying such motive outside the field of direct and familiar observation.

This sort of surplus is characteristic of Fisher's earlier poetry: after a poem's shape and closure have been registered certain words, not specially resonant or memorable in themselves, remain as a surplus of undisclosed significance over and above the known familiarity of the scene described. Their set appears arbitrary in relation to the form achieved by closure and signifies, I suggest, the position of the observer under the contingency of his own set of attention and sensibility, while at the same time it defamiliarises the contingent, recognisable world the poem has described. But this is defamiliarisation not by making strange but by making other: the contingency of the observer admits the contingency of the world observed. It is between these two positions that the surplus of signs is produced. But if there is a textual surplus, a surplus of signs – the effective local denotation of those signs notwithstanding – there is equally a surplus of reference that allows what was observed to stand free of its description. One implication of this is that for Fisher description is cognitive rather than perceptual: it employs signs not to examine sensation but to investigate what can be known.

It will be clear by now that identity, selfhood, subject position, the status of the observer and what is observed, take on a special salience in Fisher's work. With this in mind I will return briefly to the comparison of Fisher and Larkin to note a basic difference in their rhetorical procedures in order to dispel any lingering doubts about Fisher's literary competence of the sort raised by Davie. In Larkin the separation of logic and rhetoric is assumed in a typical and unexceptional way; he also wrote at a time when imagery was commonly accepted to be the dominant sign of the poetic. In his mature poems the figurative is ostensibly subordinate to propositional discourse, but is nevertheless the effective sign of literary status. There is thus a rupture within his poetic discourse as a whole, inside which the literary sign discharges itself, and this implies an absence of rupture between propositionality and reference; the poem is sealed back on to its reference and its truth guaranteed: 'this is how it is' with a vengeance. In Fisher, on the other hand, the propositional and the figurative don't have this snug demarcation (hence Fisher can be sarcastic but is not, as Davie recognises, ironic); both contribute to the formation of the literary sign, which discharges itself across the entirety of the textual surface. Poetic discourse is not, that is to say, circumscribed by the poem's formal closure but enters the social world of signs from which the poem has been first of all produced. Truth to reality can cease to be the uncomplicated predicate of the propositional since that is no longer a discursive enclosure but fulfils itself across the gaps and interruptions which in Larkin's rhetoric are the privileged domain of the figurative. In Fisher, moreover, the formally separate identity of the poems constitutes another kind of interruption across which his rhetoric accumulates and is discharged. His readers notice the unobtrusive, sporadic but persistent recurrence of word, phrase, and motif.

In the first movement of *A Furnace* 'Get out of the pit' (from the *I Ching*) correlates with 'the black middle of the pit' ('The Six Deliberate Acts': a cinema), 'had to go into the pit, dead of pneumonia,/had to go to the pit with the rest' ('Wonders of Obligation': a mass grave), and 'the black vomit-pit' ('Barnadine's Reply': a dungeon). In the same movement 'out of' occurs again in 'I walk out of the same door', 'out of the blackness', 'out of red-brown soft-rush', and 'out of a cloudiness', and the correlation with 'out of the clay-track/out of it' ('Three Ceremonial Poems') twists back through 'the mass graves dug/the size of workhouse wards/into the clay' ('Wonders of Obligation') to 'the pit'. Similarly, 'face-fragments of holy saints/in fused glass, blood-red and blue,/scream and stare and whistle' correlates with 'Blood-red and blue glass' ('matrix'), 'They howled and shone all night' ('Rules and Ranges for Ian Tyson'), and the 'chattering and humming from somewhere else' of trolley wires at the close of 'Introit'. The motif of misplaced recognition in 'a stain in the plaster that so/resembles – and that body of air/...that's like nothing that ever was' correlates with 'the crack/under the door of this room/...has the same relation to its field/as – what?' ('Diversions'). These instances should not be read as allusions to previous poems, nor as clusters of thematically related material. They operate in terms of recurrence of signs rather than meanings, and can be taken as a variant mode of surplus, produced by accumulation rather than after-effect.

4

So far I have described textual surplus in terms of technique and formality, but I also indicated that it is associated with the way that Fisher's writing is conditioned by and discloses attitudes to the possibilities and limits of poetic discourse. Modes of surplus imply that signs ('pit', for example) are always in excess of their significance (cinema, grave, etc.) and precede it; that they involve metaphorisation of the referent; and that the mode of reference – the propositional – is the metaphor constituted itself as a sign. Or, to put this the other way round, there is no special domain of the figurative, since signs are already metaphors: the simplest empirical proposition represents first of all its own semiotic system, which threatens to absorb ostensive reference. Fisher's frequent use of deixis ('Introit' makes sustained use of this figure), along with his tactic in many poems of suppressing substantive reference ('The Trace' is a virtuoso example), are indicative of ways in which Fisher's sense of the limits of poetic discourse has governed the formal procedures of his writing.

In *A Furnace* the connections of signs, disclosed by textual surplus, are major structural agencies, at once formal and discursive. The materials fed in are constituted in the first place as signs, and their relativities and connections should not be understood as associative because as signs they already possess a given and systematic character: they are not ideas or sentiments. But here Fisher's equivocal attitude to meaning becomes an issue, for much of his material is from history, or is ostensively propositional. The sign is not exclusively linguistic, but is as well pre-linguistic – it can exist as a sign in the world. *A Furnace* involves extended reflection on the nature of signs and of cognitive enquiry: how signs are produced from sense perception but have significance that is modified as enquiry is pursued; how this variation divides signs from the contexts in which they arise, from the general cases of both the perceptual field and conventional significance. The sign thus 'rides over intention' and its singularity is multiple. It accomplishes its own identity and meaning and is at the same time invested in the world as our access to it. But if Fisher looks for meanings beyond those that have already been socially produced, his objectivity is nevertheless no more than heuristic. It has probably galled him to find his writing so consistently praised as description, a type of scrupulous realism. In *City* it is the disembodied act of observation, and the mode of subjectivity associated with it, that brings into the open the textual impasse of both versions. The scrupulous objectivity which enacts the poem's closures by a censorship of imaginative freedom brings into the open by the same token the textual inadequacy of the poem's given subject matter. In *A Furnace* revision of *City* turns on the representation of subjectivity and the status of the subject as observer, witness and, potentially, articulate presence of the city's imaginative totality. It is to the imaginative totality that *City* is unable fully to realise, to *see*, that *A Furnace* directs our attention by starting over, in 'Introit', with a reprise of familiar material.

The motif of seeing ramifies across the entirety of *City* and is complex both in the way it is deployed as a method and in its positioning as a discursive topic. There is prose both of an unattributed, generalised description (but with no use of deixis to locate the subject) and of an hallucinated intensity which requires a special mode of subjectivity, that of the 'sadist-voyeur', to validate it. Interspersed are poems in which a more conventional lyric self mediates these extremes. Sight is a topic not so much of knowledge as of the imagination, and is also the privileged relationship. Its activity becomes most tender, least alienated, when it operates in the mode of fantasy, to reveal the displaced self-image of the drunken engine driver, or the nakedness of sleeping citizens. But when Fisher, commenting on the city's provinciality, is driven to say that 'Most of it has never been seen' it is more than a wry comment on the city's vast sprawl. The passive construction intimates a coherence of imaginative responsibility that reaches beyond fantasy. It is not only that the city is a limitless, featureless, purposeless aggregate; it has never been seen whole, and this lack of imagined unity is manifested in the plethora of incoherent signs thrown off by it. The city's illegibility puts a term to Fisher's attempt to reinscribe it; with no whole or integral existence of its own its literary sign must remain an aggregate of sections and localities.

Nevertheless *City* remains, in both its versions, an attempt to see the city imaginatively and thus as a whole. But the act of its imagination is divided, revealing itself self-consciously and more typically not in the passages of scrupulous description – distinguished though these are – but in a break from the exactitudes of the given, familiar scene. But it is this very move that reveals the impasse at which the poem closes in both versions. In the 1961 version this is figured in terms of poetic futility to imply that the poem has been predicated on its own failure. In the 1969 version a different type of counter-discourse is established, in which the impasse is less textual than topical: the real and the imaginary cannot be reconciled if they are possessed of equal force. It is across this contested ground that the differential quality of the poet's seeing is displayed – either 'vicious', or 'without scorn or envy'. In the interspersed poems this dichotomy contributes to the achievement of Fisher's writing: it runs through and sustains the fragile equilibrium of 'Entertainment of War', and in 'Starting to Make a Tree' the imagination of the actual has a quality of fantasy whereby it is possible finally to assert, with no tremor of pathos, 'our tree was to be very beautiful'. But these are provisional achievements, unable to forestall the invalidity of the subject in the final paragraphs incorporated from *Then Hallucinations* (1962). The sense of exclusion ('I am not the one for whom it was intended'; 'a belief that I should not be here') works into the fantasy that it is the medium on which seeing depends that ultimately must alienate subjectivity from the physical world.

> The light keeps on separating the world like a table knife: it sweeps across what I see and suggests what I do not. The imaginary comes to me with as much force as the immediate [...] I see the iron fences and the shallow ditches of the countryside the mild wind has travelled over. I cannot enter the countryside; nor can I escape it. I cannot join together the mild wind and the shallow ditches, I cannot lay the light across the world and then watch it slide away.

This is a noble admission of failure which clarifies the notion of selfhood we have to deal with. In the prose meditations on its topography the city is presented as a palimpsest, a simultaneous spectacle of signs that fail to evoke their own history and, having 'never been seen', lacking both 'mind' and 'regard', it depends for meaning on the interpretations of subjectivity. There is an economy of rapid exchange between an unwonted self, uneasily troping and decoding those signs, and the world at large, with its entire history, in which they originate. What is signified in this exchange is both elusive matter of fact and the hidden other, historian and topographer, which speaks from within and in place of the familiar self.

Such doubling or division is the crux to which *City* continually returns in moments of maladjustment between the self as observer and as participant, obligated citizen, for observation – the sign of subjectivity in *City*, but resolutely distrustful of it in the mode of the imagination – cannot afford totality of point of view except at the price of alienation. It is just such omniscience that constitutes the unacceptable condition of the poem, and justifies Fisher's initial act of sabotage, and subsequent decision to drive contradiction to its limits; the estranged signs there for subjectivity to interpret are, as the discourse of the self, also its limit. The self may want to inhabit a single world but on such conditions it is impossible to believe in one.

5

The 'Introit' by which we enter the labyrinthine enclosure of *A Furnace* is in other respects a coda to *City*. The connection is explicitly made in Fisher's Preface: it 'identifies the poem's preoccupations in the sort of setting in which they were forcing themselves on me at the time I wrote the pieces which were to be published as *City*'. As a figure of surplus which locates the connection between the poems 'Introit' represents also the surplus of the earlier period, discovered in a 'sensation as of freedom' which is then interrogated. This 'freedom' is pointedly figured over against the impasse and limit of *City*: the light which there divided real and imaginary, day and night worlds, is here itself divided, and the world thus becomes visibly one.

old industrial road
buildings to my left along the flat
wastes between townships
wrapped in the luminous
haze underneath the sun,
their forms cut clear and combined
into the mysteries, their surfaces
soft beyond recognition;
and as if I was made
to be the knifeblade, the light-divider,
to my right the brilliance strikes out perpetually
into the brick housefields towards Wolverhampton,
their calculable distances
shallow with detail.

Freedom may remain a sensation subject to qualification, a matter of 'as if', but here nevertheless a genuine freedom has been won from the limit of *City*. Against the city's lack of symbolic order the subject here registers the 'as if' purposive organisation of the suburban street down which he travels. The mind participates actively, and the input of data bears the familiar rhythm of the pulse beat. Signs no longer order themselves in opposition to the commonplace, nor does their interpretation require the alienation of the familiar self. 'Introit' opens on to the history of *City* to allow something else to emerge. It travels by trolleybus through the outskirts of the *City* landscape in order to investigate knowledge of the familiar, but also prepares the release of the subsequent movements of *A Furnace* from the epistemic boundaries of deixis. The empirical sequence of the journey is constructed cognitively and poetically not by the logic of time and space but as a series of signs that detach from their given setting as they approach and recede.

> Something's decided
> to narrate
> in more dimensions than I can know
> the gathering in
> and giving out of the world on a slow
> pulse, on a metred contraction
> that the senses enquire towards
> but may not themselves
> intercept. All I can tell it by
> is the passing trace of it
> in a patterned agitation of
> a surface that shows only metaphors.

That surface is as much the mind's as the world's, the signs traced by the senses affording direct knowledge of neither mind nor world. The form taken by the 'gathering in and giving out' is that of a curve distended around the enquirer, its curvature represented textually both locally, in the section of 'Introit' sequenced from 'Tang of/town gas' to 'a message in dark empty holes, USE GAS', and across the whole of *A Furnace* from the light 'without rarity' at the start of 'Introit' to the 'thin clear light' at the end of its seventh movement. The enquirer's 'passive taking-in' of what 'will have itself understood only/phase upon phase' is counterpoised, of course, by what is actively given out and composed by the writing, while what is understood discloses the meaning of signs in relation to the timing of the 'separate/involuntary strokes' of the mind. The mind's own internal sequence, 'dark/swings of a fan-blade/that keeps a time of its own', is now what separates signs and meaning from the extensive logic of space and time, but the mind depends for its self-representation on the signs that travel between the world and itself. Mind and world are not homologous, but occur as a particular conjunction through which signs travel thick and fast, 'many modes/funnelling fast through one event'. In this apparitional world there exist no suspended moments of contemplative insight, for meaning is always approaching and receding along the curvature of intention; like the trolley wires, always 'chattering and humming from somewhere else'.

If Fisher is not philosophically realist no more is he nominalist; he is not concerned with real existences as such but with the signs they make and by which they can be evoked. Nor, for all his play with the enquiry of the senses, is he sensationalist, for that would route him back to realism. He sets limits to the mind's reflexive knowledge of itself, and is not interested in the unconscious: underground places, dives, tombs, pits, are part of the world's disclosure and its system of signs. Whatever surfaces on the mind is not a sign of an identity locked away. His interest in knowledge concerns cognitive modes rather than positive knowledge, and he sees its boundary fluctuating with intention. The laws of the Newtonian universe – of the heavy industrial processes, and the markets they served, that lie in ruin throughout the poem – fail to describe the involution of time and space in the mind's conjunction with the world.

A Furnace develops curvature against itself in the figure of the double spiral, 'a form which enacts', Fisher says in the Preface, 'the equivocal nature of the ways in which time can be thought about'. Its seven movements 'proceed as if by a section taken through the core of such a spiral'. This graphic suggestion should not be expected to have great explanatory power, any more than the title of the poem itself; both are metaphors for the pattern of vertical movement through which signs are produced and transformed. The relation of sign to pattern, the actively changing character of knowledge, and the conjunction of mind and actively changing world, are more accurately seen as the trace of something that 'breaks/from stasis...and slides/directly and fast on its way, twisting/aspect of the torsion of the flow', or the 'nature, travelling fast,/laterally in broken directions, shallow/spinning' which 'in an instant is gone/vertically on a plunge, on a sudden/switch of attitude...plunges unaltered,/slips away down/in twisted filaments'.

In the poem's seven movements signs are composed with a freedom that breaks loose from the empirical constraints tested in 'Introit'. They range from simple residues, traces, surface agitations – the surplus of process and interaction – to entire landscapes transparent to the transformations they undergo through time. Writing is not to divide signs from their situation but to design the pattern of their correlation across established boundaries of the conceptual order.

The straight way forward
checks, turns back
and sees it has passed through,
some distance back and without knowing it,
the wonderful carcass,
figurehead or spread
portal it was walking,
walking to be within;

showing from a little distance now its
unspeakable girdering, waste cavities,
defenceless structures in collapse; grey
blight of demolition without removal,
pitiable and horrific;

the look that came forward and through
and lit the way in.

What does this describe? Is it an abandoned demolition site or a shambles? Perhaps, in the light of the lines that precede it, it is a defunct industrial civilisation that could exceed its ordinary limits to become something 'visibly not itself;/but something' as occasionally as a stud animal is put to service. The affiliation and spread of signs across the poem cannot be localised by such questions, though they help to gauge the metaphoric pitch of Fisher's imagination. In this passage 'way', 'turns', 'passed', 'through', 'walking' and 'in' connect by textual surplus with 'Staffordshire Red', and through 'cleft' and 'cut' in that poem the connection with 'pit' is made yet again. Here checking and turning back mark a break with a previous epistemic model (to be found in the very early poem 'Linear', as well as the much later 'Releases') in which things encountered in the world are thought of as swinging into place ahead of the mind's forward march, and then dying away behind. Knowing has become passage or entry rather than advance, an elementary tropism of the subject, to be realised retrospectively, so that time does not so much flow backwards as distend spatially.

This imaginative freedom is brought about by a shift of attention from the discovery and formation of signs to their mode of action, connecting across the boundaries of mind and world whenever they are not instruments of a given discourse. Fisher's most resolute revision of *City* occurs thus in the reference to 'the annexation frames/of a world that thought itself a single colony', reversing the need in *City* 'to believe I live in a single world'. In *City* the imaginary disrupts the allegiance felt to collective reality, and its action becomes self-consuming; its surplus components – light, knife, wind, ditch – finally connecting in *A Furnace*. That collective realism then becomes the city's fantasy life: 'Once invented, the big city/believed it had a brain; Joe/Chamberlain's sense of the corporate/signalling to itself with millions of disposable/identity cells, summary and tagged.' The retrieval of the imaginary is realised throughout *A Furnace* as a making of identities through the action of signs when not subjected to authority, the authority above all of time, and their making is seen as accomplishing an entry into nature. Fisher's Preface is most explicit – and can afford to be because the concept is stubbornly elusive – in its acknowledgement of a debt to John Cowper Powys 'for such understanding as I have of the idea that the making of all kinds of identities is a primary impulse which the cosmos itself has; and that those identities and that impulse can be acknowledged only by some form or other of poetic imagination.'

6

I have stressed the primacy of the sign, and its ambivalence – contingent and systematic at the same time – to show how the imagination acts textually in *A Furnace*; I hoped also to show its active, mediating character, which the text both represents and reproduces, and the mode of discourse produced by the deployment of signs within a textual economy of surplus. But this can do no more than test the conviction that the poem is not, as some readers might find, a disjointed phantasmagoria of reality but is, indeed, a coherently imagined whole. What is imagined – the timeless identities entering nature – might yet give even well-disposed readers pause. And I think we should at least pause to ask if *A Furnace* does not arrive, finally, at a heterodox mysticism. Is its aim to annul the natural fact of death? To offer a prospect of transcendence? I would argue against such readings because the poem provides no sign for transcendence as such, no self-adequate symbolism: its signs operate across multiple contexts of significance. Entry into nature is the metaphoric territory equally of Renaissance magic and the streets of Fisher's childhood; it is also 'encoding/something perennial', so that there can be no knowledge outside that of signs. To enter nature is to enter an economy of signs is which value is not equivalence. Furthermore, the poem's signs are pitted against those of an authoritarian and indifferent politics with which they dispute the nature of the lived world. But the crucial demonstration comes in the clarification of identity, and the careful placement of what is specifically human, with which the poem concludes.

The final movement of *A Furnace* approaches revelation without abandoning the agency of the sign: 'We knew they existed, but not what they'd be like;/the visitation is the form that whatever/has been expected but not imagined takes/for the minutes it occupies now.' Signs of identity are relative to time, not the threshold of timelessness. Here 'they' are clouds:

rising from behind the ridge, gigantic
heads lifted and proceeding along it, sunset-lit,
five towering beings
looking to be miles high,
their lower parts hidden, their lineaments
almost stable in their infinitely slow
movement.

Relationship is imagined textually in the way 'visitation' is counterpoised by 'materialization'. These beings may be godlike, 'perfect to themselves/in some other dimension' – the dimension of human expectation and awe perhaps – but 'they can take on only the shapes/the terms of materialization impose.' This check to and of the imagination runs both ways. These 'Creatures of the Last Days' may just be clouds, signs of atmospheric conditions, but such naturalisation can be reversed, as it is in the closing section of the movement. Natural things, snails and wild fennel, elude the value equivalents, the annexation-frames 'infest' and 'road', of the social discourse by which they are initially given.

They infest
                    the wild fennel

that infests the verges of the road
through what have become wide
spaces above the bay.

The snails ascend
                                the thin clear light,
taking their spirals higher;
                                          in the dusk
luminous white, clustered
like seed-pods of some other plant

Weeds and pests have *turned* into light and space.

Bracketed between these opening and closing sections, which reproduce the entry-and-return of the double spiral, is the human. When clouds materialise 'The human eye/watches them shrewdly, albeit/with the awe it's been craving; sizes them up,/how to ride them.' In such exchanges human qualities are needed and revealed: 'There have always been/saucers put out for us/by the gods. We're called/for what we carry.' In 'Diversions' a woman puts out saucers of milk for a stray cat, 'with his enormous guilt/and importance'; twisted through textual surplus 'guilt and importance' are rewritten as human 'hunger for action' which 'understands itself/only by way of its own//secretion, fluid metaphysical carrier/that makes, where it collides, cultures,//and where it runs free, myth.'

The stress on human agency may seem light but the statement is major: the signs that encode identity and culture originate in the same human desire, and by that desire we are attached to the world. And although the stress is light it is carefully placed, for the final movement is anticipated by surplus in the second movement, 'The Return', which reads proleptically, or as if we might read the poem not by taking a section through its double spiral but by following its entering and returning curve. Here the action of the sign that 'breaks from stasis' is what 'fetches the timeless flux/that cannot help but practise/materialization', and 'fetches/timeless identities/riding with the flux with no/determined form, cast out of the bodies/that once they were, or out of/the brains that bore them'. Identity is inexorably human. And in this section of *A Furnace* Fisher is most fully and explicitly concerned with human complexity and the negation of identity by structures of authority. The sense of another human world, 'not past, but primordial/everything in it/simultaneous, and moving/every way but forward', which is 'always/coming out, back against the flow,/against the drive to be in,/close to the radio,/the school, the government's wars', is imaginatively embodied in the iconic presence of a living assistant of revelation.

> Massive in the sunlight, the old woman
> dressed almost all in black, sitting out
> on a low backyard wall,
> rough hands splayed on her sacking apron
> with a purseful of change in the pocket,
> black headscarf tight across the brow, black
> cardigan and rough skirt, thick stockings,
> black shoes worn down;
> this peasant
> is English, city born; it's the last
> quarter of the twentieth century
> up an entryway
> in Perry Bar, Birmingham, and there's
> mint sprouting in an old
> chimneypot. No imaginable
> beginning to her epoch, and she's
> ignored its end.

She is not just what we would call a social anachronism, for her epoch will have drawn to its close long before the invention of the big city. To write like this Fisher has ceased to be the poet of a 'quaint culture', an exile 'puzzling half a life/at the statues in the town park', for he has read the signs for what they are and made them speak.

-o0o-

Crozier's interest in the Apocalyptic poets of the Forties was registered very clearly in his review of J.F. Hendry's A World Alien *for* PN Review *in 1982.*

-o0o-

Review of J.F. Hendry's A World Alien

On its front cover *A World Alien* reproduces, without identification, the street plan of central Glasgow. The river Clyde, bisecting the urban grid, is bridged and bordered by it. The configuration of reciprocal structures is immediately familiar, even if unrecognised, as the type of the centre, now decayed, of a great city. This is the place to which the poet has returned from post-war employments in Europe and North America; retired from professional life his poetic career is gathered and renewed from home. The ambiguity of the title ranges with expressive and destructive power throughout the book, reaching further to confront what must be becoming a familiar cultural type, which a younger generation of poets, preoccupied with the relation of its discourse to social life, might consider exemplary: the career in which the salaried lifespan figures as a hiatus, an unaccountable lapse which threatens to overwhelm the poet in retirement with the indignities of premature historic status. Neither past nor present affords a familiar world, and the poet's estrangement invests him with a rootless singularity. To characterise Hendry in terms of such a type, however, and not rehearse the outline of his career as it reaches back to the late Thirties (privileged treatment which with some courage *A World Alien* does not solicit) would place too close a constraint around the diagnostic ambiguities implied by the title of this modest collection of verses which spans upwards of thirty years. Self-appraisal is not primary here, although the passage of time and death are frequently observed; what the poems attend to are the altering qualities of existence in relation to the sites and contacts which institutionalise it, and beyond that their concerns open on to questions of identity and fate where the familiar is over-ruled: 'All I meant to do / was give back to you / what the world denied – / your right to die / your own destiny!'

The book asks to be read as a unified collection rather than as selected poems, and is gathered into four sections: Scottish, Love, Political, and Medieval Poems. Thematic distinctions, in the first two sections especially, are not always strongly marked. There is no indication of when the poems were written, and stylistic differences, which might offer clues to dating, cut across all four sections. Images tend to recur from poem to poem with a degree of conceptual autonomy: the face, the mirror, glass, rock, gold, sun, coin, a man with a gun. Readers familiar with the 'Apocalyptic' manner of Hendry's two wartime volumes will find instances of the same dense, highly figured rhetoric, the elements of which metamorphose rather than stabilise; a rhetoric which, for all its refusal of common sense, denotes an imagination resolutely impersonal, and conjures with intimations of historical and collective pathologies. In these poems Hendry's writing is at its most flexible and uninsistent, using the line end to effect complex syntactic readjustments within an informal grammar of complete utterances. Other poems use correlated stanzas to different, ostensibly more controlled, ends: syntactic parallelism surveys aspects of a theme in subordination to its dominant motif; an epigrammatic habit generalises itself to produce poems of two and three stanzas implying dialectic and synthesis; spatial organisation across the page sets out in a manner which assumes that bits of language retain meaning in isolation from their relations within the whole in which they occur. What resists the sense of diffusion of effect which all this variety might occasion is the inclusive ambiguity intended by the book's title; it pivots on the equation between the poems of love and politics: the love of the alien and the politics of the world. The topics of the four sections into which the book is divided are not contingent; Scotland sites the poet's affections and nostalgia, the politics of love envisages a humanity set not towards ends but within presence, 'the constant *concept* of light/as an image to be *reached*/is already a turning away from the blessing/of Being/bathed in eternal light!', figures for which are implied by the remote and simple pieties of medieval poverty and humility.

The language of politics, for Hendry, is so split with paradox as to be virtually closed to the imagination. The right words occur in the wrong mouths: '"You have free will!"/said the man with the gun'. (These lines are quoted from 'In Time of Paradox', the first of the Political Poems, and it should be noted that in this poem lines 3 and 4 have been reversed in printing, as have lines 7 and 8.) The politics of power and mass has engulfed both person and ethical discourse, in the same way that the individualism and scepticism of the seventeenth century, sanctioning the usurpation and distribution of the personifying icons of autocracy in the name of the people, have produced a politics of demagoguery and fanaticism. The image of deposed authority circulates on money, the object of envy reassigned a multiple value; signs of the division of the vitality of sun and wheat are not possessed, instead 'the biscuits became stale sovereigns and shrank into the banks'. It might appear that Hendry is being ultra-royalist here, but I think it comes closer to the mark to suggest that he is considering the nature of a state which purports to confer upon its individual subjects the autonomy of the absolute potentate. There is a correspondence of sorts between the assassinated conscience and the executed king, but Hendry is more extensively concerned with the repressed or victimised, unpossessed dimensions of existence. Hendry's politics does not give rise to an inclusive discourse; it impinges on his poetry, but his poetry is not, finally, situated within it. Those of the Political Poems not concerned with the anatomising of bourgeois and totalitarian states point, not to an alternative politics, but towards the inexpressible: the self-immolation of Laureo de Boseis's solo demonstration against Fascism; withdrawal to the desert purity of crystalline springs; 'The Massacre of the Innocents'. What stops 'For Laureo de Boseis' being a celebration of romantic individualism are the fact of his death, and the attachment of tragic dimension not to the extinction of De Boseis's life but rather to the lives of his compatriots whose small wretchedness confirms the reality principle of their state.

But if politics does not define the discourse of *A World Alien* its diverse actuality serves to interpret the psychic life of the person as citizen. Hendry's Love Poems are internal dialogues between the violent and the victim, the will and the repressed life of the person. The title poem, which refers indirectly to the 1950s sex-murderer Peter Manuel, is the most ambitious exploration of this trope. The notion that sexual assault is violence directed against the self is not new; the poem is not primarily concerned with a specific pathology, however, but searches instead to plot the ambiguities of its title, suggesting that they are ambiguities of relationship, most powerfully active when relations with the other are curtailed and refracted back into the self. At bottom, it would appear, Hendry is indicating the pathological condition of the autonomous person within a politics of power. Certainly, his world alien inhabits or is a habitation possessed by a landscape or psyche formed by the passage of an unparticipated history. Love transacts itself in isolation, internal and dismembered, as in *Hamlet* or Braque's *Still Life with Severed Head*.

It is difficult to avoid the conclusion that Hendry uses ambiguity to write at large about his relationship with his own world, using dramatic, epigrammatic and logical forms to elaborate and organise discursively in a way not afforded by his characteristic lyricism. Whereas *The Orchestral Mountain* (Routledge, 1943) and *Marimarusa* (Humphries, 1978) were essentially examples of extended lyric sequence, incremental developments of a single theme, *A World Alien* is a collection of elements organised around an implied conceptual structure. Some risk is entailed that the book will be read only as a miscellany. It also might be objected that the organisation partakes too much of an absented will, coercive in its inclusion of some of the better individual poems, and perhaps fabricating others to sustain the discursive momentum of the whole. It has, after all, often been held against Hendry that his work is over-theorised. But it is also arguable that the loose thematic ordering of the book, topic fitting within topic, reflecting and translating one another, prefigured in a way by the book's cover, is fully in keeping with the 'Apocalyptic' rhetoric which characterises still the best of these poems. Compare two versions of the first stanza of 'Inverberg', one of the Scottish poems, the first from *A World Alien*, the second from *Modern Scottish Poetry* (Faber, 1946):

1

Through the lilting mist, aglow
with rivers of restless pebbles where pocked
and speckled moss and the centuries grow,
a mountain breaks like Mosaic rock,
sliced with shade and scarred with snow.

2

Sliced with shade and scarred with snow
A mountain breaks like Mosaic rock
And through the lilt of mist there flow
Restless rivers of pebble, pocked
And speckled, where moss and the centuries grow.

There are important differences, although they are not the main issue: the pebbles have been made more literal, they no longer flow; epithets have migrated and become more resonant, the centuries themselves becoming pocked and speckled; the stanza develops more steadily towards a climactic violence, its details more fully integrated and none sagging between powerful opening and closing image clusters. More to the point, however, is the degree of similarity persisting between the two versions; extensive rewriting has been possible, barely constrained by the stanza's formal requirements, but the substance remains virtually unchanged. This can occur because the syntax binding the images together is extremely loose, governed largely by the apposition of participial phrases, and because epithets appear to be felt not as adjuncts of substantive figures but as image-components with discrete potency. Put this another way, and say that rewriting here is more exactly a matter of rearrangement, and a correspondence becomes clear: *A World Alien* is an arrangement and invention just as 'Apocalyptic' rhetoric is an arrangement of language invented as imagery. Behind all this, but at some remove, is the influence of Ezra Pound, I'm sure, although the materials his poetry arranges are very different, and rather more wilful.

Hendry's poems are the work of a complex, absorptive mind, and treat language much as that mind appears to treat its contents, by intensifying focus rather than expository order. For this reason I feel that, despite any interpretation that *A World Alien* bears as a whole, my preference for specific poems, many of them found among the Scottish Poems, in which Hendry writes closest to personal experience, has justification. Read in isolation these poems nevertheless retain the scale of reference and feeling drawn up and expounded by the book's organisation. 'Hunterston, Ayrshire', for example, a recent poem about return and loss, historical decay and haunting presence, combines the objective and value in a way which, finally, annuls ambiguity.

VIII
'FREE RUNNING BITCH'

Conductors of Chaos, *the Picador Anthology of Contemporary Poetry, edited by Iain Sinclair, was published in 1996. The radical nature of this venture was emphasised by the editor in a letter sent to all the contributors:*

> It is perfectly clear now that the conglomerate publishers can't fit such books into their standardised production-line procedures. These will have to be circumvented by the energies and strategies of the poets themselves (so that the corpus of small press/samizdat publications previously and currently produced by these poets – and the many others who could as easily have been included – can slipstream on this freakish moment of exposure).

Crozier's contribution to this venture was twofold. First, he introduced a selection of eleven poems by J.F. Hendry, emphasising the sense of the retrouvée*:*

> Forgotten poets of the 1940s can seem like pretty much an open secret, with enough collections now in print for readers to make their own conjectures about the topic, but unless as an obscure Scottish poet (he is not in the recent Faber anthology – an omission not to be regretted since he was not a poet by regional affiliation) Hendry has been largely forgotten. He was briefly celebrated during the early 1940s for his identification with the Apocalyptic school, but didn't achieve notoriety during the subsequent reaction against what the Apocalypse was taken to represent, and by then what the Apocalypse had seemed to stand for in poetry had dissolved, through over exposure, into a generalised neo-romanticism. Dylan Thomas still has to take the rap.
>
> Hendry can be important for us today because of the kind of poet he was; so saying, I do not discount the value he has as part of an ignored or forgotten history (for, of course, open secrets remain secret). His poetry ran in parallel with an intelligent and thorough cultural and social critique which was elaborated in a series of essays during the late 1930s and the 1940s; that in itself is striking enough, but it is not the important point, for the connection between critique and poetry was not theoretical: neither was

> subsidiary to the other; both remained separate activities in their own distinct domains of intelligence within a single project. These essays were timely interventions in a world facing collapse, the same world his poems confronted; they offered a critique of mechanical system based on the role played by myth in the behaviour of societies and persons. Man himself was a myth which reason could not justify. Hendry's poetry, in its unconscious derivation, corresponds to that part of his critique which denies the concept in favour of an *episteme* of the image.
>
> Apocalyptic writing, Hendry argued, broke through strictures of language and social convention and offered both diagnosis and cure. It revealed the chaos of normality in order to address human value. We are not, I think, to understand his poems as apocalyptic by virtue of their imagery, even though it signifies a world of collective ruin, separation and violence, or if we do, we merely describe a mode of contemporary pathos. That is the risk his poems incur. But they aspire to more than this, to present to us an image in which we may feel and understand the chaos of history and its sources in us.

His second contribution to the volume was his last series of poems, 'Free Running Bitch'. In the first issue of the Cambridge Literary Review *(2009), Rod Mengham pointed to this last sequence as 'a movingly complete statement of the formal and conceptual cohesiveness that can be achieved by an experimental poetic':*

> The movement of the poem is one of urgency, no loitering, yet it starts by coming to terms with deceleration, with the space-time continuum of a managed environment encircling both traffic queues and hospital queues. It thinks about the difference between queuing and waiting, the latter 'like stopping for/time to think,' open to improvidence and improvisation, the former regulated, planned, inflexible.

The poem was reissued in Star Ground *in 2008 as a Silver Hounds publication, where it was placed beside 'The Veil Poem' and 'Star Ground', a late poem dedicated to Crozier's wife, Jean. In a series of tapes made by Crozier just before his death he made it clear that the 'Free Running Bitch' sequence was the poem of which he was most proud. When asked the reason for this he replied that it was because it was about landscape, about a dog; that it repeats itself and is set over a period of time. It was about hospitals, his mother, his father in hospital, his wife in hospital; it was about dogs running in woods; it was a poem about family life, science, things that happen.*

-o0o-

Free Running Bitch

1

Believe it. But I won't. He stayed in May
followed by June. Soon, poetry in slow
motion, queues in traffic, like stopping for
time to think, stopped in the same queues,
not the same, at the same time,
more or less, in the same place (what
did he think?) Would I believe it,
it's in the diary. No, it's on notices.
In the year planner, in several year planners,
it's colour coded for a month, and the month
after: knowable frequency equations
for different colours. No such signal
for stopping, neither poppies, nor ragwort,
on headland, in pasture, nor the cornflowers
cornflower blue. But the red, the green
under yellow. Amber? Wait here, it says, there,
Sorry for any inconvenience. He knew that
processing frequencies for colour tends to
equalise with spatial percepts from
retinal data. Believe it or not,
he knew that, wrote it under (summarised)
World History Notes, forgot it, forgets when.
Stops the car, the car in front
red, stationary red, or metallic grey,
metallic stationary grey, or as soon moved
some yards as kept its distance, he'd stop
or move forward all the same coloured spaces.
I'd include ragwort with Danger Don'ts, not forgetting
to walk on the footpath, if there is one.
(There was.) Everyone remains seated.

2

Good to arrive at verges, let all
reflections shine, their light absorbed
and the proper colour of grass a bit
smudged, pressed one way and smeared
to look oily, skid mark of a heavy body
fallen; the warmth of the sun in patches,
sky mottled with clouds, all the changes
as good as random: what next, shall we
go on or shall we stay as we are, and
how much longer? Orange glints and
goes dull, intensity varies along the
line which gives a surge here and there
then settles down. Movement erratic at
any point, points for contingent reference
only. You like this mess? That's a tame
comparison in the wild, I don't reckon
its chances, no but flutter unconvinced
for all the good it does. There's just the one
and we've got it, or don't believe it,
you've had that. Want some more? Subtract
backwards, divide through zero, your share,
amass a fraction of history. I'm not
waiting either, just sitting here looking,
what's there doesn't move much more than me,
and I'm not moving at all relative to
what's in front; what are they doing if not
fixing barriers and kerbs in concrete, fitting
inspection covers on drains? Moved you look
away, but it's the same window, put up your
soap box for a viewing platform. Go on.

3

Looking up from his well-thumbed India paper
World's Classics *War and Peace*, time he read it
again, was half my greeting. Half asked me
what I did there. Assured he would send for me
were there occasion, what was I up to
disturbing you reader? In the next bed,
all of them made up and empty but for another
whose occupant slept behind screens, the one

opposite, in fact, hospital cornered
occupied or not, under his eye (his book
half to read, half read) he had, kept it on,
one who (are there such characters in it?)
at all times, all days, all through the regime
of starched nursing bodies, received visitors,
all of them women. They arrange business.
There like a man surrounded by women –
they are many and it's something like
bigamy – he sits marking the place reached
again in his old blue favourite Tolstoy,
Oh to the life, in my life. Why should he
or I be appointed with reasons for
living, for absences as rare and as
good as happen to anyone? In bed
there, away from the windows, wanting
for nothing, he finished his book and quietly
went home. Things he'd not asked for
weren't to be had where crowds throng
and jostle in shops, the familiar and
unaccustomed streets, where we ate
and drank, and I began to read.

4

My car was right outside, more or less
lined up beside the wall those windows look
through, rows of them, one storey above another,
illuminated, scarcely lighting up the autumn evening
but opening out of it, interiors to exclude
visitors, get them out of their cars
disoriented, after a circuit of the site
in search of a space, walking along an access road.
Locate that curtain wall broken with lights.
The hospital closing round those admitted,
assuming all needs, and those drawn to it
hesitate, approach and scatter at random,
in search of a way through. To join in. They
imagine wants and their fulfilment defines
a covert urgency to mark the occasion and
claim it. No gifts exchanged but there are
things to remove, dispose of, return fresh,

replace. All this going on, behind all those
windows, looking for a door, signs, corridor
off some stairs, someone finally picked out
and greeted: different here, of course, strange,
still not part of it all. Temporary. Short
stay. Ignore the others. Stigma of
no visitors. Not thinking at all of this
looking for a space and remembering where
to find it, locking and leaving the car,
walking beneath the glow of many windows,
leaving the evening outside for the vast
bright illimitably self-contained interior
I arrived and could see my car outside in the gloom.

5

Red and white alternate in bands, say they
are stacked or tapering segments, the line
of the stripes curved around less pronounced
than an outline of rod or cone which jumps
from figure to ground filling in gaps,
section to plane, volume with shape as bodies
in space set out in rows to start looking
repeating itself, recessional accent on memory
making out lines between stripes run around
and all over, see them flash by, time unit
continuous for two frequency cycles, heart
stutter, one travelling fast round another's
light pulse, delayed burst, in the sequence and
out, remnants of colour displayed, falling
away on the curve of its tangent, out of
the corner, scattered before its return swept
into the bay as a double beat counted twice,
its point in the line divided and dotted
back where, see what, time rushing past
your one body, small corner and one little eye,
time rushing ahead through its gaps, meeting
its markers and dying away as you pass,
snatched up to the stars, sideral passenger,
so many vertices plotted, invisibly now,
across the celestial sphere, so much infinity
sectioned, such stories foretold, fixed a word

for them, call it out luck, or under what sign,
or on what base are they struck, short use life,
weather beaten, fallen, degraded, one on its own
if not lost must have been stolen.

6

Some things I've had for years, like her old
exercise book. Hay loads in trusses, rods of brick
work measured cubic feet. Out of the window by her
bed we looked on to an artificial lake, curved round
the angle of two wings, a few rushes planted
and some mandarin ducks, all too soon
for Spring. Oh, and weren't there
a couple of pubs on this road we sometimes used.
From the imposing car park through the vestibule
where a few people, some of them in nightgowns,
sit at café tables, the way is clear and easy.
After that it's a place of echoes. Her new
sketchbook. The woman in the bed opposite –
here, I've done some drawings, she always has
her head swathed in that shawl – must know she's
so odd-looking, and I've tried not to let her
see me. The pages turned past landscapes and
foreign buildings and opened to let us glimpse
her strange neighbour; no views of the new
made parkland, only the sky out to sea
appears across the tiled window ledge.
These books? Favourites brought by friends
who visit, I might read some of them. They're
not people who read. Not her exercise book old
through disuse, its ruled feint lines still a blank
history of the world, covered in red like
an old globe for imperial infants with
warnings on traffic, tables for everything, and an
illegible map of home. Don't run, don't pass,
don't play, don't follow, don't hang on, don't forget.

7

Madrid, and so on, *Britons in Spain*, she
can go now: spirit of old battlefields,
intense and passionate. Break some bones

in Ronda if you must. Fall on the stones.
Is the heart not the life, he enquired, of
long male memories; she thought something more
recent, little house and steps up to it,
little feet overheard advance and retreat
impatient for a loved face, I saw her
at once and exclaimed. Stone echoes follow
feet running past to cheat eloquence in
flight and take off after mother, there
he goes, dad's parked the car again. Straight forward
returning, hardly the rites of passion
in situ, nor so subtle as friendship,
without wheedling phrases, no fussy talk
about feelings, just a grunt, just his way
with words in public. Where I'd put in the
phrase, not dressing it up like, dog's dinner,
she has to say how cold he is, and numb,
and so on, married again, no more the
single parent of her orphan children,
and but for her he'd say his dumbness spoke
from the heart for stone. Observe his silence.
Watch the phone. Throw the starving dog a bone.
Folie à deux grows dog-eared, like romance,
everything, like nothing, wants permission
under exclusive contract – who does the
shopping, who stays home – it's a weak ending
no full stop. She rang, he ran. Both hung up.

8

Plants, animals, anachronous arrays
of information, let's be strict about it they're
too early; keep the curtains drawn against
those cries hurled against the breaking light,
let it break ever so evenly I've no envy.
It's an epistemic intervention
she wants to see with, or to light her dream
a modern knowledge of spectography.
Give us the light falling uniformly
white to appear shiny and fresh, your bare
minimum attributes and a quality
surface, she maintains colours as entities

down to earth. She's so go-ahead, you old
stick-in-the-mud, ours but as we are
whatever we see in them. Take also
natural light, if not an element
it's a problem to apply, keeps dividing
presence from absence by partial absorption,
unseen except in its various weathers
(as incompletely above. The forecast
is different.) It's a thought I heard her lisp
Shall we join them, their skin tingles and glows
with its heat in these photos, Oh much less
than in Winter, and I'm stung by that quite
tender pink of her lips as they tremble
and spill. Then she went upstairs and he cried
right out, and heard his tears hiss on the grate.
She read that in her book, try it even
if you never want the assurance of
your own fundamental identity.

9

This is almost cosy – what's for dinner?
Also temporary, like any difficulties
with cards and flowers. Here are more
of both. I can stretch out on your bed
not being you, you can keep to the easy chair
in easy reach, or I can take the upright
across from the invalid table. You prefer
upright, the table between us. From there
on the shelf and any spare surface
there are the bouquets and pot plants
and the cards. How cold and slow they said
you were in the recovery room; after that,
recovered, there was nothing to reassure about you,
no trim coverlet and restful pillow,
endured in your wrap of fatigue you shrank
shockingly in the bedside chair, all of you
puckered up, in your nightdress and
dressing gown, pain outwardly visible.
Then you opened your eyes. Terror was gone
and you began to speak like a survivor
of the terror of unconsciousness, the terror

of awakening, and what lay between,
the line of sutures from your sternum tightening
into your armpit. The next day all the
magazines had the same story, suddenly
your story, lives saved and lost, yours
saved again. Soon the way you came in
will look strange, opened out backwards, your return
preceded by flowers, the car to be full of them,
but now watch the racing from your vacant bed.

10

Lost from sight where planting and cleared scrub
give on to the ride, a plantation to the right,
opposite, unmanaged coppice bolting skywards,
but her bell heard, its tinkling travelled ahead,
stopped for a while, starting up deeper in, approaching,
stopping again: to go in or keep walking,
past a path cut into coppice down which
disturbed standing water reflects tops and sky,
across rising ground, woods and open sky divided,
at its crest severing treetops upright,
over its shallow ridge and straight on,
the ride reaching ahead, to a plank thrown over
a ditch, sunk in the clay, yellow ditchwater
lapping its face, where, after crossing, to
wait, or not, if having come out of the wood, free
running bitch, she ran after, impossible to miss
her continual jingle, or if waiting to hear her
bell as she runs to catch up, or still tinkling
in the wood, or no sound for minutes, then the
shook flap of her ears: to stand and wait, hunker down,
or follow the sound in, criss-cross between the quick
slender growth and fallen trunks, angled branches,
see her head down follow her nose through bracken
and bramble and vanish, broken outline of variegated
fawn and white slip through dappled light,
bell notes startling elsewhere, the air traced
by her passing, parting of trails sniffed
quickly, hear her panting breath louder
on the scent of exhaustion after some hours
of this, see, she returns on tentative bloody feet.

Star Ground

For his wife

Difference of coarse and fine
The abrasion of the sky
Snow drifts along the hedge
In plumes and spurs

At ground level
Swept clear and bare
Ice chips like glass

Light scatters on dry gusts of air
Shrinks and breaks apart

Frost heaves all night
To rise like waves
Spent on the margin
On the enduring
Particular resistance of our love

-o0o-

Crozier published very few poems in the last twelve years of his life, although he was clearly working on drafts of some. One notable exception was 'Blank Misgivings', his contribution to the magazine Gare du Nord *(volume 1, number 3) edited by Alice Notley and Douglas Oliver in 1998. In 2004 the poem was reprinted in* Vanishing Points: New Modernist Poems, *edited by Rod Mengham and John Kinsella. The debt that 'Blank Misgivings' owes to Wordsworth's phrase 'The Child is father of the Man' is manifested in one of the many drafts of this late poem, which has 'W.W. "My heart leaps up…"' at the head of the manuscript and which contains the note: 'The father in the child is the model of the child's future – not an inheritance but a prophecy of the child's mortality in terms of the father's'. Crozier had played with the possibility of calling the poem 'Scraps of Comfort' and 'Obstinate Questionings' before settling upon its final title.*

-o0o-

Blank Misgivings

Our father death speaks through the child our father
the sailor lost beside a dream of immense steppes
perfectly rigged violets inside a sunken bottle
tears condensed beneath the clear glass in the path

O fly you creatures, asiatic cranes and gazelles
slender ribbed of arctic birch and whalebone
air twists into grey sheets of old starlight
the extinct hiss of incendiary in a bombed cellar

This morning's trace of footprints leads back where
sidereal years modelled in spars and struts
thrust from the ground, stumps of brickwork
a broken corner where the sky turns cold

Remember such things under the new city
shadows of ruin swept into unlit night
one bare horizon drawn across another
day into day breaks the calamity of the heart

What to call to out of ignorance and loved best
the abrupt twilight and the unexpected dawn
when brief cries summon falls unanswering voice
pauses between the echoes of the century

Listen to the wagons thunder and the static roar
light outlined burning through the grid
the abandoned garden and the tumbled fence
alike and other unbuilt monuments to hope

The stones rest as they fall, the dying fall
among the dead and I could wish their bones
at rest their day so what there was each find
so be it the unhoped-for be no more than man

IX
RESTING ON LAURELS

Crozier's essay 'Resting on Laurels' appeared in British Culture of the Postwar: An Introduction to Literature and Society 1945–1999, *edited by Alistair Davies and Alan Sinfield and published by Routledge in 2000. According to a letter Davies sent to Crozier after receiving the first draft of the piece, 'The collection is designed for first-year undergraduates and after – those who don't study poetry at university (largely, as you say, because their tutors know little or care little about it).' The ongoing battle which Crozier fought against the poetry-publishing world had been recognised in the late 1970s by John Riley, who wrote to Michael Grant: 'Incidentally, did you see Crozier's review of my* Ways *in this week's* Spectator? *Not quite as incidentally as all that, for the hefty bricks he therein throws at our established poets and moribund publishers might go some way to demonstrate in respectable fashion to the academics that there is a problem of some sorts thereabouts.'*

-o0o-

Resting on Laurels

Is there any reason to expect that an up-to-date account of British poetry since the war will differ in important ways, except perhaps in details of personnel, from an account of the poetry of the first twenty-five post-war years written twenty years ago? If not, then our poetic culture – represented by the poetry on view in the chain bookstores, or taught in schools (little poetry is taught, or read, in universities nowadays) – has remained largely unchanged in half a century. This essay seeks to substantiate this proposition, bringing the perspective of 1980, as it were, to bear on the last twenty years. More controversially, perhaps, it will suggest how the canon has developed, and adapted, sustained by the discursive habits that encoded it as poetic language at the moment of its inception in the 1950s, in a period in which poetry has moved yet farther away from the cultural centre. The reason for this is obvious: as an economic activity poetry is marginal, just as is, for example, hill farming. No one wishes to admit this, least of all publicists of the contemporary canon, but the behaviour of publishers demonstrates it as matter of fact. On the one hand, less and less cultural capital accrues from subsidising poetry: the place of poetry in the culture industry is increasingly specialised; on the other hand, and this is the more telling point, even a modestly profitable poetry list is likely to be axed because of its insignificant position in company balance sheets. Taking poetry as an economic activity, I would hazard the guess that – the occasional best-seller notwithstanding – its most lucrative sector is the secondary market, operative in the rights departments of publishers, and the 'modern first' trade. (It is commonly thought that royalties from Lord Lloyd-Webber's *Cats* are what have kept Faber & Faber a going concern.)

1 *'Thrills and Frills'*

In a glibly titled essay (to which this section title refers), published in Alan Sinfield's *Society and Literature 1945–1970* (1983), I suggested that a canon of contemporary poetry had developed in the 1950s and 1960s, and cited Philip Larkin, Ted Hughes and Seamus Heaney as its foremost representatives, establishing each in turn a poetic succession from decade to decade. This was hardly contentious then, nor is it now. I proposed that despite polemic disagreements on the score of gentility, in which a poem by Hughes might be held up as significantly of the post-war world and serious, in a way that one by Larkin, by virtue of its nostalgia, was not, the canon thus constituted was homogeneous. And I argued that this homogeneity consisted in those common features of canonical work – its discursive habits – that constituted it as poetry: the enunciation (as we've learned to say) of an empirical subject, and a textual insistence on figures of rhetoric as the discernible sign of the poetic. That is to say that these two features, which are related, were (and, I shall maintain, still are) generally understood to be the necessary conditions of a poem; that is to put it at its best. At the worst they were (and are) its sufficient conditions.

The relation between empirical subject and rhetorical figuration is the canon's defining nexus, in which what is figured is given as deriving from the posited experience of a self which, in turn, appears as the author of the poem's figurative scheme, in a discursively foreclosed writing. Imagery does all the hard work of the poem, subject to ratification and guarantee (as fit for consumption) by an originating self. This is true equally of Larkin, Hughes, and Heaney, so that whatever their genuine differences – which are, as much as anything, a matter of temperament, inflections of an individual poetic 'voice' – they represent and define a canon of contemporary poetry with determinate horizons of social and cultural engagement and, I might add (for I think these the more important), no horizon at all for engagement with either the history of poetry as an art, or the questions of metaphysics and ontology that concern us as human beings which great poetry has addressed. This is increasingly inevitable while poetry is represented as belonging to or, indeed, bearing responsibility for a national culture. This is not strictly an issue of specific national identity, and Heaney's objections to being enrolled in an anthology of 'British' poetry were personal to him. To the extent that poetry belongs to culture (as of course it does) and culture is not exclusively national (as it never has been, despite the pretensions of the nation state) a canonical poetry identified by reference to national identity (however problematic that may prove) will be a poetry that has reduced its scope of human concern. The canon itself, being a critical and cultural construct, cannot be held responsible for this, needless to say, but the purpose of such constructs is to command assent, and the consequence of uncritical and unreflecting assent regarding the properties that constitute a written item as a poem is an instrumental logic of cultural production to standardised specification. A poem is recognisably *thus*. So our poetic culture is more than ever a matter of figuratively embellished anecdote. But whereas, in the immediate post-war world, there may have been reason for poets to wish to be seen as meaning to stand by their words, to assume responsibility for their role in an aesthetic discourse towards which they felt distrustful, we cannot suppose that reason still to apply with any urgency. Indeed, whatever reason applied, it was in the aftermath of the illusion that poetry might exert direct social agency. Auden, of course, had dealt with that issue succinctly and with equanimity when he said that poetry made nothing happen.

In its account of the canon that began to be established in the 1950s my essay paid particular attention, of course, to the 'Movement' poets and the canonical anthology *New Lines* (1956), in the Introduction to which the editor, Robert Conquest, had explicitly argued for the rediscovery of a native tradition of poetry, in repudiation of a modernism that was essentially foreign, as well as various subsequent aberrations of the 1930s and 1940s. Conquest's irritable polemic misled, by its demand for a return to basics, and failed to disclose the motives, typical of the Movement poets, towards a disparagement of affect, low-key irony, and themes of thwarted expectation. That there was an ethic in all this, attuned to the post-war moment, no one can doubt, and what it conveys to us in the best of them, Larkin himself, and Donald Davie, is a subjectivity formed around not so much self-denial as dismay. To articulate an ethic as poetry requires that writing a poem be itself considered an ethical activity, undertaken with a display of self-conscious control if that ethic is a predicate of the private person, and poems as I have described them to be constituted in the canon are apt for the purpose, but composition in such a mode, once the purpose of which it is formally significant has ceased to obtain, leads to disequilibrium: without the pressure of the ethical subject the tropism of figurative rhetoric becomes its own end. I thought this was to be seen already under way in Larkin's successors, first Hughes, then Heaney (and down, I suggested, to Craig Raine): their poems were different from those of their predecessors only in the sense that their motivations were no longer the same, but were nevertheless poems of the same kind, and were treated accordingly in a somewhat cursory fashion. In an equally cursory manner, but by way of contrast, I drew attention to poetry of other kinds, giving as examples specimens of writing by Charles Tomlinson and W.S. Graham: poets of quite different types, chosen because, although scarcely of the canon, both had received a modest amount of public attention. In both, I argued, the place of the subject was vacated in favour of, so to speak, an objectively grounded and embodied experience.

My assessment of Larkin and Davie, in particular, would probably now be more generous than it was, perhaps because I am better able to recognise in their reluctance, hesitation, and dismay the signs of their ethical dilemma as poets, and what they took to be the ethical dilemma of poetry in the post-war world, despite the suspicion that this was rather conveniently assumed on the basis of a tendentious construal (caricatured by Conquest) of the high art tradition in the Twentieth Century. (To do proper justice to Davie, he also went on to write with impressive eloquence in non-canonical modes: the verse epistle, for example, and what can best be described as the disrupted symbolist lyric). This sense of dilemma was not shared by all British poets, least of all perhaps by those who felt an affinity with other poetic traditions, and it was helpful (and still is) to recall Tomlinson's phrase of sharp reproof, in a review of *New Lines*, since it applies with equal force both to what Tomlinson thought to be its poets' 'suburban mental ratio' and what I have discerned as their posture of ethical responsibility. Tomlinson also spoke, with more acuity than we should expect given his sneering reference to the suburbs, of the Movement poet's 'mental conceit of himself', and this is telling because reflexive self-conceit can take more than one form. What Tomlinson identifies as a 'suburban mental ratio' may well correspond to what I have inferred to be an assumed ethical dilemma, but that is not the issue, for his acuity lay in discerning the character of a poetics in which the mind of the poet is manifested as a mode of self-reflexivity. Given the ethical bearing of Tomlinson's own poems (that of the serious artist, mindful both of knowledge and its objects and their energies) we should not be misled by his recourse to an ethical terminology of personal qualities. At issue is not that poets are conceited (they mostly are, anyway), but the direct representation in the poem of the poet's controlling intelligence – or personality, idiosyncrasy, obsession, whatever it may be. To be blunt about it, Tomlinson's objection to the Movement poets was that they expected readers to be interested in reading about *them*, an objection that applies by extension to the entire contemporary canon. Moreover, Tomlinson's phrase might be turned around to apply equally to the reader's own 'mental conceit of himself', to make the point that our canonical poetry is designed to establish the reader's empathetic identification with the figure the poem gives of the poet.

The argument being repeated here, by which it is maintained that there exists a canon of poetry defined not so much by the excellence of the poems as by the fact that they are inclusively of the same sort, may appear, because of its persistent totalising of post-war poetry, vulnerable to fundamental objection on matters of detail: either that the poems of the canonical poets are not of this sort, or that poets whose poems are not of this sort belong in the canon. Of these the former is the weightier objection, and I shall go on to discuss an instance of it provided by David Trotter. The latter type of objection will most frequently be encountered as a quibble, indignation that a favourite poet has been somehow slighted. Objections of this sort are an attempt to have one's cake and eat it, for the truth is that a canon exists in a nebulous hinterland, as the cultural property of a host of minds and institutions, comprising both poets and poems, and will manifest itself thus as virtually *given*. The canon that I identified twenty years ago was, in effect, either given to me, or adopted by me from an ambient culture, and I recall no dissent from the flat assertion that Larkin, Hughes and Heaney exemplified it. Just because of its nebulous existence a canon must also be able to be represented as a strongly outlined construct. Is Davie canonical? Probably not, though some of his poems probably are, and the question is not one we ask when thinking about Davie's work, or any other poet's, on its own terms.

In a review of *Society and Literature 1945–1970* Trotter suggested that the period under review did not allow my case to be fully made since my canonical poets 'were beginning, around 1970, to write in ways that challenged the projection of a mental conceit on to the world'. The allusion was to my use of Tomlinson's phrase, of course, minus the crucial element of reflexivity. My riposte might be that Trotter had not fully ascertained the nature of my case, which concerns poems rather more than it does 'the world'. But this would just be a point scored against a critic who had interesting things on his mind that bear on what I have to say. In *The Making of the Reader*, published in the same year as his review (1984), Trotter devoted a chapter to what he discerned as beginning around 1970, using the terms 'pathos' and 'anti-pathos' to frame what was now different, but offering it as no more than a 'significant although perhaps temporary, change of emphasis'. (That qualification, I infer, was due to hindsight.) The opposition of pathos and anti-pathos placed Larkin and Heaney under the first category in a separate chapter, and I merely note that there the 'pathos of subjectivity' is glossed as 'the responsibility to say what one feels about things' – and that is close to the the imperative to be seen as standing by one's words. Anti-pathos, on the other hand, represented 'an opportunity for English poetry which is now in some danger of fading' – obviously since two of the three books that stood for it, Hughes's *Crow* (1970), and Geoffrey Hill's *Mercian Hymns* (1971), had proved to be blips in their author's careers. Trotter at least had the consolation of being able to say, in the case of his third exemplary book, that the author of *Brass* (1971), J.H. Prynne, 'has not followed the later Hughes and the later Hill back to the pathos of origins'.

Trotter's categories may strike athwart my notion of the canon, but they do not marshall the evidence to controvert my case. Quite the reverse, in fact. On his own evidence, there was no significant reorientation of the canon after the 1960s: indeed, the canon was strongly reinscribed in the 1970s, as Heaney came to the fore. *Crow* and *Mercian Hymns* were, in their way, exceptional, but as slapstick fictions, light relief for otherwise dour temperaments. Nevertheless, *Crow* strikes me as a prime example of the canonical sort of poem in a particularly etiolated manner, for surely Hughes's fictive persona is principally characterised, down to his acts of self-erasure, by his mental conceit of himself. Hill, on the other hand, I would not claim for the canon; he has his admirers, but they are too strong-minded to bother with that kind of thing, while his poetry is too recusant to be co-opted. And furthermore, Trotter's concluding chapter, taking its evidence from, on the one hand, handbooks for teaching poetry in schools and, on the other, from the poems of the 'Metaphor Men' (Craig Raine and the poets associated with him as 'Martians') found him drawn to the baleful conclusion: 'Comparison, one of the many different ways in which poems signify, has become a sign for poetry itself: for the entire scope and value of the art.' But while I agree with this, as a statement about the canon, I obviously don't accept his suggestion that this may be a consequence of the way poetry is taught in schools; there may be an element of feedback, but the phenomenon is immanent to the canon itself. The figures of rhetoric (to which comparison is fundamental), in the argument I have advanced, conferred poetic authenticity on Movement poems, under the vigilant superintendence of the ethical qualms of the Movement poet, but their role in this transaction did not confer on them any prestige, since poetry itself was (given its recent history) an object of suspicion. In other words comparison was already the sign for poetry itself. Take away those qualms and the canon lets rip, for a time at least, in the way Trotter described. But we should not lose sight of its capacity to turn in a different direction, towards a poetry of mental self-conceit.

2 *The Canon Rests on its Laurels*

I proposed at the outset that our post-war poetic culture has remained largely unchanged, and in the course of reviewing a former argument about the canon of poetry to 1970 I suggested, in passing, that the canon was geared to assumptions about its status as representative of a national poetic culture. I maintained that the canon to 1970 comprised poems of a particular sort, a poetic discourse which had once answered to specific cultural and social imperatives but which, with their passing, persisted as the exclusive sign of the poetic. My proposition now requires, therefore, arguments to show that the canon to 1970 has extended down to the present. It will not be enough to challenge anyone to deny that Larkin, Hughes, and Heaney retain exemplary canonical status, or that they are still read in terms of the poems that established them thus, even if the longevity of their esteem tells in favour of my case.

But in reviewing my diagnosis of the canon to 1970 I also anticipated, of course, the case that now requires to be made. Although Heaney began to publish, to acclaim, in the 1960s, his exemplary prominence belongs to the 1970s. the same is to be said, moving on a decade, of Craig Raine, who began to publish in the 1970s, but whose general *reclame* was a thing of the 1980s. This is going over ground already covered, but it throws light on how the canon obtains as a cultural construct. For a start, while it persists as such, the canon will remain posited over against the poetries that antedate its 1950s inception. It will not invite us to reconsider modernism, or the poetry of the 1930s, yet alone that of the 1940s. Indeed, the excesses of the 1940s come to be reduplicated in recent canonical polemic as the excesses of the 1960s. On the other hand, what the canon excludes of the recent past is less than ever represented (as it was by Conquest, for instance) as that which might constitute its other. Thus the occluded past can become a site of ad hoc and whimsical recuperations and fetishisings: of Auden for example, or that perennial adolescent standby, Weldon Kees. These are signs of the canon's diminished poetic vitality, as were its raids farther afield on poetry behind the Iron Curtain, or the texts of ethnopoetics. This lack of vitality is offset, to an extent, by the spectacle of the entropic energy of the canon itself: younger poets are now less interested in the question how to write than in the question how to publish. The former question has, for practical purposes, been settled since we have a canon in which poetry is a fully socialised cultural product. But because poetry's position in relation to cultural production and consumption is eccentric, at the very margin, it can afford no more than a handful of canonically definitive poets (more likely to be read about, than read, in the culture at large, their names a litany of reproach to a reading public that thinks perhaps it ought to read some poetry). Defined thus, the canon extends over time by accretion of new names, at the rate of one per decade: from the 1950s, Larkin; the 1960s, Hughes; the 1970s, Heaney. For the 1980s, I've suggested Raine; and for the 1990s, surely, the definitive poet has been Simon Armitage.

When I suggested, twenty years ago, that the canon to 1970 'extended itself' in the work of Raine, it was merely to indicate the lie of the land: a prospect of poets being 'praised above all else as inventors of figures', and a canon falling yet more spectacularly into decline. The coincidence of my view of the poetry of the 1980s with that of Trotter, nevertheless, is merely confirmation of part of the evidence for the case that Raine's poems are of the canonical sort. In *Contemporary Poetry and Postmodernism* (1996) Ian Gregson took issue with me on this point, wishing to show 'the extent to which' poets such as Raine had 'broken with the tradition of the

Movement'. The metaphorised textual economy of Raine's poems was not in dispute, but he alleged (citing Bakhtin) that their 'structural principle is the interaction of points of view' rather than 'image-making'. (This, I am afraid, will prove to have given the game away). Thus while Gregson agreed with what I said about the role of the self in the Movement, he supposed that he could transfer that intact in order to refute its application to Raine by claiming that 'the Martian poetic…systematically undermines the authority of the self by restlessly enacting the vulnerability of its knowledge'. On the one hand, Gregson did not take the force of my point that figures of rhetoric 'constitute the nature of the poem', which applies equally to Larkin and to Raine; on the other hand, he failed to notice that in my argument about the continuity of the canon there was an inverse relation between the authority of the self qua subject and the efflorescence of figures of rhetoric. Furthermore, his assertion about Martian poetics, which connects back to his notion of interaction of points of view (how this can be a 'structural principle' in the lyric quite eludes me) was simply wrong. Metaphor can only work if the identity of its terms is recognised: Martian poetry, therefore, far from existing in a state of epistemological uncertainty can be wonderfully periphrastic because it is cognitively certain of itself. More to the point, Raine is certain of, indeed complicit with, his reader's ability to identify what is not mentioned by name – typically by transpositions of visual scale. As Trotter put it: 'In Raine's world, a packet of cigarettes looks like a miniature organ and a rose has a shark-infested stem.' Even if, as in his signature poem 'A Martian Sends a Postcard Home' (1979), Raine represents his figures of rhetoric as originating from a cognitive set unlike ours, unfamiliar with the names of things in our everyday normality, it is far-fetched to situate such misprisions as implied dialogue, as if the poet had encountered an authentic other, whose rather precious figures of rhetoric he bore no responsibility for. To the contrary, the very attempt to project another consciousness, another point of view, by means of the figures that define the text as a poem, seems self-defeating. Raine is a master in his 'Martian' house. For myself, I'd prefer my martian more like the real thing. 'Sit ka vassisi von ka, sta'chi que v'ay qray'.

Gregson and I differ because he eschews any concept of poetry, of what constitutes something as a poem. Like most of our poetry critics, he takes whatever is handed to him on a plate and makes the best of it. No one will mistake a Martian poem for a Movement poem (not even me), their differences are clearly marked, like tabby and tortoise-shell cats, but Gregson wishes to differentiate them radically, on the basis of their different styles of subjectivity, and must indulge in fanciful hermeneutics to justify this, whereas I discern their radical identity in the textual role of the subject both inscribe.

If Raine does not represent a break with the canon inaugurated by the Movement, but instead is its beneficiary, what are we to make of the claims recently made on behalf of a new generation of poets of the 1980s and early 1990s, showcased in the 1993 anthology *The New Poetry*, where Armitage appears to figure as its terminus ad quem? This anthology was quickly followed by a complementary volume of essays by one of its editors, David Kennedy, *New Relations: The Refashioning of British Poetry 1980–1994* (1996), complete with an Appendix 'The New Poetry – A User's Guide' giving 'pointers on using The New Poetry with GCSE and Advanced Level examination syllabuses for 1996 and 1997', and was already in its fifth impression by 1996. This smacks of genuine success, and Kennedy's subtitle pinpoints the editors' claim that their anthology documents a cultural shift. That Kennedy also recuperates this new poetry for the national culture might then seem tactless, given the editors' anti-centrist claims in view of which, we might well ask, what is this poetry doing on the curriculum? Well, it 'emphasises accessibility, democracy and responsiveness, humour and seriousness, and reaffirms the art's significance as public utterance'. That is to say – the editors are somewhat impressed by the novelty of this – it is self-consciously politically concerned: 'poetry and political concerns...are inseparable'. It is post-imperial, post-colonial, multicultural, pluralist, devolutionist, provincial, anti-authoritarian, and generally bien pensant. What we can all feel comfortable with, each in our own social exclusion zone. In effect we are invited to read this new poetry as a return of the repressed (culturally speaking); an outburst from the hitherto silent majority oppressed by the cultural and political system. In this populist arena for confused-identity politics we are, it becomes apparent, solicited to read their poems for the poets' mental conceit of themselves.

But this is largely window dressing, including a lot of excess baggage that Kennedy smartly drops from his exposition of an inclusively *British* poetry in *New Relations*. Out (but for impeccable reasons) go the Irish and Afro-Caribbean poets, and women poets are denied a separate look-in – a surprising ecumenical gesture, since while the Afro-Caribbeans went because they are 'still being theorised', the same can hardly be said of writing by women. This clears the ground for a traditional configuration of British poetry, but with a grudge against the English class system, particularly as manifested in the 1982 *Penguin Book of Contemporary British Poetry*, explicitly the *terminus a quo* for *The New Poetry*. Whatever its overt politics *The New Poetry*, seen in its true colours, is a foray into the village politics of British poetry, based on a shrewd appraisal of both the canon and its history and, as such, a bid for centrality and cultural legitimacy. This is implied by its editors' choice of title, claiming for their anthology affinity with A. Alvarez's 1962 anthology also entitled *The New Poetry*, which effectively subsumed the Movement's codes of discourse while denouncing the gentility of English cultural tradition in order to extend the hegemony of the canon. *The New Poetry* (1993) situates itself toward *The Penguin Book of Contemporary British Poetry* precisely as *The New Poetry* (1962) situated itself toward *New Lines*.

Kennedy's historical case runs something like this. Larkin by his example had sanctioned a degree of contemporary realism, which in the next or 'middle' generation became the privileged frame of reference. Kennedy presents this realism in terms of communities inhabiting a landscape that is a 'blighted urban pastoral of...industrial froth and dismantled cars', while its cultural bearing relates to 'issues of access, ownership, property and rights'. The poets of this generation speak back, as it were, to their sponsor Larkin, from marginal communities acknowledged in his poems but unknown to them. They also prepare the ground for poets of the next generation, represented by *The New Poetry* (1993), whose individual voices both continue the struggle with the central culture and its class position and, because that struggle has been won, represent a release of the poetic imagination into the pleasures of mass culture. This is both and at once an argument about ownership of the canon since the Movement, and a claim for historical and political significance. Thus it can be suggested that we are to see in this history some reflection of the break-up of a post-war consensus, and that the new generation's consciousness was forged politically within Thatcher's Britain. But what seems to me more striking is that these arguments based on exclusion are belated, for they belong to the 1950s, when they were urged – very convincingly, since they then could cite a widespread turn to realism – with reference to the theatre, cinema, and the novel. It might be countered that it is poetry that is belated (though these same arguments were once held to relate to Larkin), but that would be to miss the point, which is that these arguments ascribe to the institution of poetry a cultural authority and oppressive agency inconceivable in late twentieth-century culture. But the fiction that this is so lends legitimacy to the struggle for centrality, for possession of poetic culture, which turns on the correct representation of the 'middle' generation. For while the 'middle' generation of poets who speak back to Larkin from the social margins his poems glance at, Douglas Dunn, Tony Harrison, and Heaney himself (who can seem like the joker in every anthologist's pack), are represented in the *Penguin Book of Contemporary British Poetry*, their place there was usurped and instead Raine's Martianism and the 'secret narratives' of Andrew Motion and James Fenton were enthroned. Thus the anthology is seen by Kennedy as an attempt to draw a veil over the radical credentials of the 'middle generation' by claiming its continuity with the poetic mainstream, invoking postmodernism in order to separate it 'from a wider cultural, political and social context'. Dunn and Harrison, and Peter Reading (whose exclusion from the *Penguin Book of Contemporary British Poetry* so scandalises Kennedy), may well be forebears of the next generation's mental conceit of itself, but it is easier to detect in them a staged immiseration and the self-pathos of the elective outsider than a convincing politics. Nor is it credible to suppose that metrical verse represents, in their hands, a political gesture of cultural expropriation; rather, it serves to foreground an aestheticised disgust.

These arguments do not have to persuade in order to be successful as a tactic for establishing the poetic centrality of the next generation's new poetry drawn from the socially excluded margins, and both Armitage and Glyn Maxwell are now safely with Faber & Faber, publishers to the canon. Of the two, Armitage is by far the more frequently spoken of, and he is by virtue of that representative of his generation, and also representative of the canon by virtue of the sort of poem he writes. He serves therefore to close my case. Whereas in Raine the discursive subject is axiomatically the poet, there as the originator of a steady drip of metaphoric events, the Armitage persona is somewhat various, but invariably demotic, an average citizen or common man. This is the poet who is like his readers to the extent that they don't normally read poetry, and are pleasantly surprised that it deals with routine stuff of everyday life: probation officers, football, drugs. Discursively, that is to say, Armitage's poems are directed by an intransigent fiction of the ordinary person. So far so good. But these ordinary people, it turns out, possess a transformative imagination attuned to remote comparisons, and can speak like Raine's Martians. In 'You May Turn Over and Begin', for example, the straddled legs of a female pillion rider, suddenly sans motorbike, resemble a wishbone; in 'B & B' a dead mole is both like a pocket and like a purse; in 'Parable of the Dead Donkey' an empty grave fills with rain like a bath. Such poetry was new only in the sense that it was waiting to be recuperated by the canon, prime cuts resting on Movement laurels.

SELECTED BIBLIOGRAPHY

Poetry

Loved Litter of Time Spent, Buffalo, NY, Sum Books, 1967
Train Rides, Pampisford, Cambridgeshire, R Books 1968
Walking on Grass, London, Ferry Press, 1969
In One Side & Out the Other (with John James and Tom Phillips), London, Ferry Press, 1970
Neglected Information, Sidcup, Kent, Blacksuede Boot Press, 1972
The Veil Poem, Providence, RI, Burning Deck, 1974
Printed Circuit, Cambridge, Street Editions, 1974
Seven Contemporary Sun Dials (with Ian Potts), Brighton Festival, 1975
Pleats, Bishops Stortford, Hertfordshire, Great Works Editions, 1975
Residing, Belper, Derbyshire, Aggie Weston's, 1976
Duets, Guildford, Circle Press, 1976
High Zero, Cambridge, Street Editions, 1978
Were There, London, Many Press, 1978
Utamaro Variations (with Ian Tyson), London, Tetrad, 1982
All Where Each Is, London and Berkeley, CA, Allardyce, Barnett, 1985
Selected Poems, in *Ghosts in the Corridor*, London, Paladin, 1992
'Free Running Bitch', in *Conductors of Chaos* (ed. Iain Sinclair), London, Picador, 1996

Books edited

A Various Art (ed. with Tim Longville), Manchester, Carcanet Press, 1987; London, Paladin, 1990
Poems 1923–1941 by Carl Rakosi (ed. with an introduction), Los Angeles, Sun & Moon Press, 1995
Poems and Adolphe 1920 by John Rodker (ed. with an introduction), Manchester, Carcanet Press, 1996

Articles

'Fielding Dawson's Prose', *Kingfisher* (University of Sheffield), 1976
'The Young Pound', *PN Review*, 6, 1977
'The World, the World: A Reading of John Riley's Poetry', in *For John Riley* (ed. Tim Longville), Wirksworth and Leeds, Grosseteste Press, 1979
'American Photography', *Journal of American Studies*, 14.3, December 1980
'Thrills and Frills: Poetry as Figures of Empirical Lyricism', in *Society and Literature 1945–1970* (ed. Alan Sinfield), London, Methuen, 1983

'Inaugural and Valedictory: The Early Poetry of George Oppen', in *Modern American Poetry* (ed. R.W. Butterfield), London, Vision Press, 1984
'Styles of the Self: The New Apocalypse and 1940s Poetry', in *A Paradise Lost: The Neo-Romantic Imagination in Britain 1935–1950* (ed. David Mellor), London, Lund Humphries, 1987
'Signs of Identity: On Roy Fisher's *A Furnace*', *PN Review*, 83, 1992
'Hope and Distrust', *PN Review*, 88, 1992
'Carl Rakosi in the Objectivists' Epoch', in *Carl Rakosi, Man and Poet* (ed. Michael Heller), Orono, ME, 1993
'Paper Bunting', *Sagetrieb*, 14.3, February 1997
'Zukofsky's List', in *The Objectivist Nexus* (ed. Rachel Blau DuPlessis and Peter Quartermain), Tuscaloosa, University of Alabama Press, 1999
'Resting on Laurels', in *British Culture of the Postwar: An Introduction to Literature and Society 1945–1999* (ed. Alistair Davies and Alan Sinfield), London, Routledge, 2000
'Carl Rakosi and the Library of America', *Metre*, Spring 2004

Selected secondary material

Ackroyd, Peter. *The Collection*, London, Chatto & Windus, 2001. Two reviews of pamphlets by Crozier. 'Some Little English Versifiers', pp. 18–22, contains a review of *Printed Circuit* (this review first appeared in the *Spectator*, 4 January 1975). 'Verse, and Worse?', pp. 32–6, contains a review of *Pleats* (this review first appeared in the *Spectator*, 20 December 1975).
Allen, Tim, and Andrew Duncan. *Don't Start Me Talking: Interviews with Contemporary Poets*, Cambridge, Salt Publishing, 2006.
Brinton, Ian. 'Black Mountain in England: 4', in *PN Review*, 169, 32.5 (May–June 2006). Online: http://www.pnreview.co.uk/cgi-bin/scribe?file=/members/pnr169/articles/169ar06.txt.
Brinton, Ian. 'Underneath the Arches: Some Comments upon Andrew Crozier and Charles Tomlinson'. *Tears in the Fence*, 49 (Winter 2008/9), pp. 82–93.
Brinton, Ian. 'Andrew Crozier 1943–2008'. *Eyewear*. Online: http://toddswift.blogspot.com/2008/04/death-of-andrew-crozier.html.
Brinton, Ian. Review, *The Use of English*, 56.3 (Summer 2005), pp. 266–70. This review of *Vanishing Points* (ed. Rod Mengham, Salt Publishing) contains commentary on 'Blank Misgivings'. Online: http://www.le.ac.uk/engassoc/poetry/reviews.html#Mengham.
Butler, Thomas. 'Writing at the Edge of the Person: Lyric Subjectivity in Cambridge Poetry 1966–1993'. PhD thesis, University of Notre Dame, IN, 2005. Online: http://etd.nd.edu/ETD-db/theses/available/etd-06302005-113210/unrestricted/ButlerT082005.pdf. Commentary on 'The Veil Poem', pp. 63–6.
Caddy, David. 'Letter 15'.Online: http://davidcaddy.blogspot.com/2008/07/letter-15.html.

Cutler, Amy. 'Deconstructing the Map in Late Twentieth Century British Poetry'. Online: http://amycutler.wordpress.com/2009/09/15/deconstructing-the-map-in-late-twentieth-century-british-poetry/. Contains commentary on 'On Romney Marsh'.

Duncan, Andrew. *Origins of the Underground*, Cambridge, Salt Publishing, 2008. 'Andrew Crozier and the influence of the observer on the observation', pp. 70–77.

Feinstein, Elaine. 'In conversation with Michael Schmidt', *PN Review*, 118, 24.2 (November–December 1997). This interview, which contains a brief but telling comment on Crozier, is available at http://www.elainefeinstein.com/PNR-interview.pdf.

Fisher, Allen. 'Towards Civic Production', *Reality Studios*, 10 (1988). This review of *A Various Art* (ed. Andrew Crozier and Tim Longville, Carcanet Press) contains comments on Crozier's poetry on pp. 66–7, 72–3, 77, 79, 85.

Forrest-Thomson, Veronica. *Poetic Artifice: A Theory of Twentieth-Century Poetry*, Manchester, Manchester University Press, 1978. Includes an analysis of *Printed Circuit*, pp. 139–41.

Gregson, Ian. *Contemporary Poetry and Postmodernism: Dialogue and Estrangement*, Basingstoke, Palgrave Macmillan, 1996. Contains discussion of Crozier on pp. 149–50, 192–5.

Harding, Jeremy. 'Elective Outsiders', *London Review of Books*, 19.13, 3 July 1997. Commentary on Crozier's poetry, pp. 13–14. Online: http://www.lrb.co.uk/v19/n13/jeremy-harding/elective-outsiders (subscription required).

Johnson, Nicholas. 'Andrew Crozier: poet and poets' champion' (obituary). *The Independent*, 16 April 2008. Online: http://www.independent.co.uk/news/obituaries/andrew-crozier-poet-and-poets-champion-809561.html.

Joris, Pierre. 'Andrew Crozier 1943–2008'. Online: http://pierrejoris.com/blog/?p=541#more-541.

Keery, James. '"Schönheit Apocalyptica": An Approach to *The White Stones* by J.H. Prynne'. Section 6, 'The Shining One', contains a brief commentary on *Pleats*. Online: http://jacketmagazine.com/24/keery.html.

Larrissy, Edward. 'Poets of *A Various Art*: J.H. Prynne, Veronica Forrest-Thomson, Andrew Crozier'. Ch. 3 of *Contemporary British Poetry: Essays in Theory and Criticism*, ed. James Acheson and Romana Huk, New York, State University of New York Press, 1996. Discussion of Crozier on pp. 74–7.

Lopez, Tony. *The Poetry of W.S. Graham*, Edinburgh, Edinburgh University Press, 1989. Brief commentary on Crozier's essay 'Thrills and Frills', pp. 12–13.

Lopez, Tony. *Meaning Performance: Essays on Poetry*, Cambridge, Salt Publishing, 2006. Ch. 10, 'Pound and Postmodern British Poets'. Commentary on 'Free Running Bitch', pp. 143–51.

Marriott, D.S. 'The Swerves of Distance: The Veil Poem', *Archeus*, 2

(1989), p. 9.

Marriott, D.S. 'Veil, no. 2'. In *Complicities: British Poetry 1945–2007*, ed. Robin Purves and Sam Ladkin, Prague, Litteraria Pragensia, 2007, pp. 145–52.

Mengham, Rod. 'Free Running Crit'. *Cambridge Literary Review*, 1.1 (Michaelmas 2009). Commentary on 'Free Running Bitch', pp. 189–92.

Milne, Drew. 'Agoraphobia, and the Embarrassment of Manifestos: Notes towards a Community of Risk'. *Parataxis*, 3 (Spring 1993). Contains inter alia commentary on Crozier's introduction to *A Various Art* and his involvement with *The English Intelligencer*, including quotation from a letter from Crozier to Peter Riley, pp. 25–39. Also online: http://jacketmagazine.com/20/pt-dm-agora.html.

Oliver, Douglas. 'Andrew Crozier's Perceptions', *Fragmente*, 8 (1998), pp. 107–17.

Owens, Richard. Online: http://damnthecaesars.blogspot.com/2009_09_01_archive.html. Blog entry for Tuesday 1 September 2009 contains brief commentary on 'The Veil Poem', no. 4.

Prynne, J.H. Introduction to Crozier's book *Loved Litter of Time Spent*, Buffalo, NY, Sum Books, 1967.

Purves, Robin. 'What Veils in Andrew Crozier's "The Veil Poem"'. *Blackbox Manifold*, 2. Online: http://www.manifold.group.shef.ac.uk/issue%202/Robin%20Purves%202.html.

Riley, Peter. 'On Andrew Crozier's Poetry', *Archeus*, 2 (1989), p. 10.

Riley, Peter. 'Andrew Crozier' (obituary). *The Guardian*, 21 July 2008. Online: http://www.guardian.co.uk/books/2008/jul/21/culture.obituaries.

Riley, Peter. 'Andrew Crozier: An Appreciation', *PN Review*, 182, 34.6 (July–August 2008). Online: http://www.pnreview.co.uk/cgi-bin/scribe?file=/members/pnr182/reports/182rp02.txt.

Sheppard, Robert. 'Artifice and the Everyday World: Poetry in the 1970s'. Ch. 6 of *The Arts in the 1970s: Cultural Closure?*, ed. Bart Moore-Gilbert, London and New York, Routledge, 1993. Discussion of Crozier on pp. 136–7, 147–8.

Sheppard, Robert. *The Poetry of Saying: British Poetry and its Discontents, 1950–2000*, Liverpool, Liverpool University Press, 2005. Ch. 2, 'The British Poetry Revival', pp. 57–8. Online: http://robertsheppard.blogspot.com/2005_04_01_archive.html (entry for Monday 25 April 2005).

Sylvester, William. 'Andrew Crozier', in *Contemporary Poets* (6th edn), ed. Thomas Riggs, Detroit, St James Press, 1996, pp. 208–9.

Tuma, Keith. *Anthology of Twentieth-Century British and Irish Poetry*, New York and London, Oxford University Press, 2001. Brief critical account by the editor, pp. 687–8; footnotes (by Nate Dorward) to 'The Veil Poem', pp. 689–91.

Tuma, Keith and Dorward, Nate. 'Modernism and Anti-Modernism in British Poetry'. Ch. 28 of *The Cambridge History of Twentieth-Century*

English Literature, ed. Laura Marcus and Peter Nicholls, Cambridge, Cambridge University Press, 2004. Contains a discussion of Crozier's essay 'Thrills and Frills', pp. 516–17.

Vincent, Steven. 'Andrew Crozier – A Little Remembrance'. Online: http://stephenvincent.net/blog/?p=637.

Ward, Geoff. 'Thy Brows with Ivy and Laurel Bound', *Archeus*, 2 (1989), p. 5. An essay looking at language in Veronica Forrest-Thomson and Crozier.

Wilkinson, John. Review of *Residing* in *Perfect Bound*, 1 (1976).

Wilkinson, John. *The Lyric Touch: Essays on the Poetry of Excess*, Cambridge, Salt Publishing, 2007. Brief comments on *Pleats* (p. 122) and 'The Veil Poem' (pp. 88, 183–4).

INDEX OF POEM TITLES

INDEX OF POEM FIRST LINES

INDEX OF NAMES